OPPOSING
VIEWPOINTS®
SERIES

# Behavioral Disorders

# Other Books of Related Interest:

**Opposing Viewpoints Series**
Health

**At Issue Series**
Mental Illness and Criminal Behavior

**Current Controversies Series**
Mental Health

"Congress shall make
no law . . . abridging
the freedom of speech,
or of the press."

*First Amendment to the U.S. Constitution*

The basic foundation of our democracy is the First Amendment guarantee of freedom of expression. The Opposing Viewpoints Series is dedicated to the concept of this basic freedom and the idea that it is more important to practice it than to enshrine it.

## OPPOSING VIEWPOINTS® SERIES

# Behavioral Disorders

*Louise I. Gerdes, Book Editor*

**GREENHAVEN PRESS**
*A part of Gale, Cengage Learning*

Detroit • New York • San Francisco • New Haven, Conn • Waterville, Maine • London

GALE
CENGAGE Learning

Christine Nasso, *Publisher*
Elizabeth Des Chenes, *Managing Editor*

© 2010 Greenhaven Press, a part of Gale, Cengage Learning.

Gale and Greenhaven Press are registered trademarks used herein under license.

*For more information, contact:*
Greenhaven Press
27500 Drake Rd.
Farmington Hills, MI 48331-3535
Or you can visit our Internet site at gale.cengage.com

For product information and technology assistance, contact us at

Gale Customer Support, 1-800-877-4253
For permission to use material from this text or product, submit all requests online at www.cengage.com/permissions

Further permissions questions can be emailed to permissionrequest@cengage.com

Articles in Greenhaven Press anthologies are often edited for length to meet page requirements. In addition, original titles of these works are changed to clearly present the main thesis and to explicitly indicate the author's opinion. Every effort is made to ensure that Greenhaven Press accurately reflects the original intent of the authors. Every effort has been made to trace the owners of copyrighted material.

Cover Image copyright Dvirus, 2009. Used under license from Shutterstock.com.

**LIBRARY OF CONGRESS CATALOGING-IN-PUBLICATION DATA**

Behavioral disorders / Louise I. Gerdes, book editor.
   p. cm. -- (Opposing viewpoints)
   Includes bibliographical references and index.
   ISBN 978-0-7377-4502-3 (hardcover)
   ISBN 978-0-7377-4503-0 (pbk.)
   1. Behavior disorders in children. I. Gerdes, Louise I., 1953-
   RJ506.B44B435 2009
   618.92'89--dc22
                                                           2009025837

Printed in the United States of America
1 2 3 4 5 6 7 13 12 11 10 09

# Contents

## Chapter 3: How Should Behavioral Disorders Be Treated?

# Why Consider Opposing Viewpoints?

> "The only way in which a human being can make some approach to knowing the whole of a subject is by hearing what can be said about it by persons of every variety of opinion and studying all modes in which it can be looked at by every character of mind. No wise man ever acquired his wisdom in any mode but this."
>
> *John Stuart Mill*

In our media-intensive culture it is not difficult to find differing opinions. Thousands of newspapers and magazines and dozens of radio and television talk shows resound with differing points of view. The difficulty lies in deciding which opinion to agree with and which "experts" seem the most credible. The more inundated we become with differing opinions and claims, the more essential it is to hone critical reading and thinking skills to evaluate these ideas. Opposing Viewpoints books address this problem directly by presenting stimulating debates that can be used to enhance and teach these skills. The varied opinions contained in each book examine many different aspects of a single issue. While examining these conveniently edited opposing views, readers can develop critical thinking skills such as the ability to compare and contrast authors' credibility, facts, argumentation styles, use of persuasive techniques, and other stylistic tools. In short, the Opposing Viewpoints Series is an ideal way to attain the higher-level thinking and reading skills so essential in a culture of diverse and contradictory opinions.

In addition to providing a tool for critical thinking, Opposing Viewpoints books challenge readers to question their own strongly held opinions and assumptions. Most people form their opinions on the basis of upbringing, peer pressure, and personal, cultural, or professional bias. By reading carefully balanced opposing views, readers must directly confront new ideas as well as the opinions of those with whom they disagree. This is not to simplistically argue that everyone who reads opposing views will—or should—change his or her opinion. Instead, the series enhances readers' understanding of their own views by encouraging confrontation with opposing ideas. Careful examination of others' views can lead to the readers' understanding of the logical inconsistencies in their own opinions, perspective on why they hold an opinion, and the consideration of the possibility that their opinion requires further evaluation.

## Evaluating Other Opinions

To ensure that this type of examination occurs, Opposing Viewpoints books present all types of opinions. Prominent spokespeople on different sides of each issue as well as well-known professionals from many disciplines challenge the reader. An additional goal of the series is to provide a forum for other, less known, or even unpopular viewpoints. The opinion of an ordinary person who has had to make the decision to cut off life support from a terminally ill relative, for example, may be just as valuable and provide just as much insight as a medical ethicist's professional opinion. The editors have two additional purposes in including these less known views. One, the editors encourage readers to respect others' opinions—even when not enhanced by professional credibility. It is only by reading or listening to and objectively evaluating others' ideas that one can determine whether they are worthy of consideration. Two, the inclusion of such viewpoints encourages the important critical thinking skill of objectively evaluating an author's credentials and bias. This evaluation will illuminate an author's reasons for taking a particular stance on an issue and will aid in readers' evaluation of the author's ideas.

It is our hope that these books will give readers a deeper understanding of the issues debated and an appreciation of the complexity of even seemingly simple issues when good and honest people disagree. This awareness is particularly important in a democratic society such as ours in which people enter into public debate to determine the common good. Those with whom one disagrees should not be regarded as enemies but rather as people whose views deserve careful examination and may shed light on one's own.

Thomas Jefferson once said that "difference of opinion leads to inquiry, and inquiry to truth." Jefferson, a broadly educated man, argued that "if a nation expects to be ignorant and free . . . it expects what never was and never will be." As individuals and as a nation, it is imperative that we consider the opinions of others and examine them with skill and discernment. The Opposing Viewpoints Series is intended to help readers achieve this goal.

*David L. Bender and Bruno Leone,*
*Founders*

# Introduction

*"Identifying an emotional or behavioral disorder is difficult for many reasons. . . . The combination of factors affecting development—biological, environmental, psychological—are almost limitless."*

*—Pacer Center, an organization that champions children with disabilities.*

If you were to ask people on the street to define behavioral disorders, you would likely get a wide variety of answers. Even among those charged with researching or treating behavioral disorders, clear definitions prove to be both elusive and contentious. Some mental health professionals include only behavioral disorders that occur among children and adolescents, such as attention-deficit/hyperactivity disorder (ADHD), oppositional defiant disorder (ODD), and conduct disorder (CD). In addition to these disorders, others include autism, generalized anxiety disorder (GAD), obsessive-compulsive disorder (OCD), post-traumatic stress disorder (PTSD), and social anxiety disorder (SAD). Still others include alcoholism, other addictions, and phobias. According to the *McGraw-Hill Concise Dictionary of Modern Medicine*, a behavioral disorder is a "disorder characterized by displayed behaviors over a long period of time which significantly deviate from socially acceptable norms for a person's age and situation."

Since Western cultures now accept as normal behavior once considered deviant, one might expect the number of behavioral disorders to have declined. However, Western cultures have also seen a shift in attitudes toward mental illness. As the stigma of mental illness has been decreasing, the number of mental disorders, including behavioral disorders, has been increasing. Indeed, behaviors that were once considered by many to be personality flaws or defects in character have now been identified as symptoms of behavioral disorders. Thus, excessive worry is not a personality flaw, but generalized anxiety disorder (GAD). In the same way, children once considered unruly and disruptive are no longer "bad" children, but may instead be diagnosed with ADHD. Closely tied to this construction of dysfunctional behavior as mental disorder is the idea that treatment is possible. Personality flaws and defects were once thought to be untreatable—part of one's character. However, modern mental health professionals believe that behavioral disorders can be treated. For example, in its fact sheet "The Myth of the Bad Kid," the Substance Abuse and Mental Health Services Administration (SAMHSA) maintains, "With understanding, attention and appropriate mental health services, many children can succeed—they can have friends, join in activities and grow up to lead productive lives." Thus, many see this shift—characterizing dysfunctional behavior as mental illness—as a positive direction for the mental health profession.

Others argue that this "medicalization" of everyday life is anything but positive. These civil libertarians often cite controversial psychiatrist and professor Thomas Szasz, who claims that most human behavior is the result of personal character, habits, and choices, good or bad. Over the years, Szasz and like-minded individuals assert, doctors have begun to classify poor choices and bad habits as psychiatric diseases that cause people to act in ways that society considers inappropriate. Szasz vehemently opposes the medical classification of behavior as disease, asserting that this classification is simply a way to control people by medicating or institutionalizing them. "Because the mind is not an object like the body, it is a mistake to apply the predicate disease to it," Szasz writes. "The 'diseased mind' is a metaphor, a mistake, a myth," he reasons. Indeed, the overarching question, whether behavioral disorders are, in fact, real mental illnesses is reflected in the debates concerning their seriousness, their causes, their treatment, and the policies that will best address these disorders.

There is a consensus among most mental health professionals that behavioral disorders are real mental disorders that have a significant impact on individuals, families, and the community. According to SAMHSA, as many as five of every 100 children have ADHD and at least one in 100 have CD. Both disorders, mental health experts argue, can have a dramatic impact on the education and socialization of those who suffer from them. In fact, these analysts assert, if left untreated, children with these disorders often end up in the criminal justice system. In addition to affected children, an estimated 4.1 percent of adults between the ages of 18 and 44 are afflicted with ADHD, according to the National Institute of Mental Health (NIMH). Those with adult ADHD have difficulty keeping jobs and maintaining relationships, putting stress on families defenders of the diagnosis maintain. The institute also claims that 2.2 million U.S. adults have OCD and as many as 7.7 million have PTSD. Since OCD and PTSD are difficult to treat, advocates argue, people who suffer from these debilitating disorders can face tremendous obstacles.

While most mental health experts agree that some behavioral disorders such as OCD are severe enough to require treatment, some dispute whether behavioral disorders such as GAD and SAD should be included in the *Diagnostic and Statistical Manual of Mental Disorders* (DSM). The American Psychiatric Association drafted the DSM for use by mental health professionals to diagnose mental disorders. While a generally recognized diagnostic tool, the DSM has met with serious criticism. The manual was first drafted in 1952. At that time, the manual included only 106 mental disorders. Since then, the DSM has been through three formal revisions. The most recent revision, in 1994, includes 297 disorders. Despite the widespread use of the DSM, critics claim, the fact remains that there is no objective diagnostic test for mental illness. Many therefore question whether the DSM categories and criteria are valid and reliable. If a behavioral disorder cannot be defined according to objective criteria, opponents reason, its validity cannot be measured. According to Szasz, "Medical classification—the linguistic-conceptual ordering of phenomena we call 'diseases' and of the interventions we call 'treatments'—is a human activity, governed by human interests." Indeed, these human interests, the pharmaceutical industry in particular, have led some to challenge the validity of behavioral disorders.

Some commentators claim that expanding the definition of mental illness to include behavioral disorders has created millions of new patients and billions of dollars in profits for pharmaceutical companies. According to Canadian drug-policy researcher Alan Cassels, "over the past decade we've seen the pharmacologizing of everyday life at a breathtaking pace—the rampant and colonizing forces of the drug industry, sometimes slyly, sometimes overtly, reshaping the normal ups and downs of everyday life and turning them into market opportunities." For example, sociologist Peter Conrad claims that GlaxoSmithKline, the company that manufactures the drug Paxil, which is often prescribed for the treatment of depression, has spent millions of dollars to raise public awareness of relatively new categories of behavioral disorders. Conrad points out that shortly after the Food and Drug Administration approved Paxil for the treatment of SAD and GAD, GlaxoSmithKline spent millions on sophisticated marketing campaigns. According to Conrad, the company created ads that include the voices of both experts and patients, "providing professional viability to the diagnoses and creating a perception that it could happen to anyone."

To some, expanding the diagnostic criteria of behavioral disorders has even broader consequences. "While the debilitating diseases of the poor—such as malaria, tuberculosis and sleeping sickness—have few or no treatments, the drug companies are busy working on cures for a ballooning set of 'made-up' diseases of the rich and privileged," Cassels reasons. In fact, the Pharmaceutical Research and Manufacturers Association itself reports that since 1995, the research and development staffs at U.S. drug companies have decreased by 2 percent, while their marketing staffs have increased by 59 percent. According to activist Angela Bischoff, who campaigns on behalf of mental health reform, the priorities of health care must change. "Instead of squandering billions on medicalizing and treating the symptoms of normal life," she maintains, "we should focus our resources on preventable and treatable life-threatening diseases."

Whether the expansion of mental illness to include behavioral disorders is a positive development remains hotly contested. The authors of the selections in *Opposing Viewpoints: Behavioral Disorders* explore these and other issues concerning the nature and scope of behavioral disorders, their causes, and how best to treat them in the following chapters: Are Behavioral Disorders a Serious Problem? What Factors Contribute to Behavioral Disorders? How Should Behavioral Disorders Be Treated? What Policies Will Best Address the Challenges That Behavioral Disorders and Their Treatment Pose? How these views will influence the way in which behavioral disorders are defined and treated in the future remains to be seen.

OPPOSING
VIEWPOINTS®
SERIES

# CHAPTER 1

# Are Behavioral Disorders a Serious Problem?

# Chapter Preface

Whether behavioral disorders are a serious problem—indeed, whether they should be characterized as mental illnesses at all—is one of the principal debates on the subject. Some claim that the increasing number of officially recognized behavioral disorders identified in the fourth edition of the *Diagnostic and Statistical Manual of Mental Disorders* (DSM-IV) is a result of increasing awareness of mental disorders and their treatment and a corresponding decrease in the social stigma of mental illness. Others argue that these disorders are not diseases at all, but normal behavioral differences among human beings. Opponents of expanding the definition of mental illness to include behavioral disorders assert that the pharmaceutical industry has turned behavioral differences into chemical diseases with chemical cures in order to increase profits. One behavioral disorder that is reflective of this debate is social anxiety disorder (SAD).

Those who believe that SAD is a serious problem claim that the disorder affects as many as 15 million Americans. While most everyone feels anxious at certain times—before giving a speech, for example, or when asking someone out on a date—according to the Anxiety Disorder Association of America (ADAA), those with SAD actually feel physically sick from fear in what most would see as relatively nonthreatening social situations. For instance, those with normal social anxiety might feel awkward when walking into a room full of strangers; someone with SAD, on the other hand, would feel too anxious to attend even a holiday party among friends. The distinction, these advocates assert, is that for those suffering from SAD, the anxiety is persistent, irrational, and overwhelming. "In extreme cases, the disorder can disrupt social lives to the point that people may have few or no relationships at all, making them feel powerless and alone," maintains Jerilyn

Ross, ADAA president and licensed clinical social worker. Indeed, according to the DSM-IV, to be diagnosed with SAD, one's social anxiety must be such that it "interferes significantly with the person's normal routine, occupational (academic) functioning, or social activities."

Critics claim that social anxiety is akin to shyness and is a character trait, not a disorder. According to Christopher Lane, the author of *Shyness: How Normal Behavior Became a Sickness*, neuropsychiatrists triumphed over talk therapists in the third revision of the DSM, turning neuroses into distinct disorders with specific symptoms and pharmaceutical cures. In fact, in his letter of resignation to the American Psychiatric Association, psychiatrist Loren Mosher said, "Psychiatrists have become the minions of drug company promotions." Mosher laments, "No longer do we seek to understand whole persons in their social contexts—rather we are there to realign our patients' neurotransmitters." Indeed, the new DSM opened the door to new conditions—what some may characterize as new niches for pharmaceutical companies to fill. Barry Brand, the product director of the antidepressant drug Paxil, told *Advertising Age*, "Every marketer's dream is to find an unidentified or unknown market and develop it. That's what we were able to do with social anxiety disorder." Ray Moynihan and Alan Cassels, the authors of *Selling Sickness*, call this repackaging of social anxiety the corporate-induced creation of disease. According to Moynihan and Cassels, "a health system that allows drug companies to play a role in determining who is sick is fundamentally unhealthy." Moreover, they maintain, "a medical profession too inebriated by the largesse of profit-driven drug companies cannot serve the public interest."

Commentators continue to contest whether SAD is a serious behavioral disorder or a pharmaceutical industry–induced disease. The authors in the following chapter explore other controversies in the debate over the seriousness of behavioral disorders.

> *"People with ADHD have difficulty concentrating and may not be able to get organized enough to begin a task, let alone finish it."*

# Attention-Deficit/Hyperactivity Disorder Is an Incapacitating Behavioral Disorder

*Linda Bernstein*

*In the following viewpoint, Linda Bernstein asserts that Attention-Deficit/Hyperactivity Disorder (ADHD) causes many behavioral problems for those who have it. The main characterization of the disorder is having difficulty paying attention, but a major problem regarding diagnosis is that many people exhibit this symptom, yet some do not have ADHD. Moreover, many people do not exhibit unusual conduct, or are bright enough to compensate for the disorder, and they go undiagnosed and do not benefit from treatment, claims Bernstein. Bernstein is a contributor to* Current Health 2, *a Weekly Reader publication.*

As you read, consider the following questions:

1. What percentage of 4- to 17-year-olds are diagnosed with ADHD, according to the Centers for Disease Control and Prevention?

2. Why might someone who has trouble paying attention not have ADHD?

3. Why is it important to have an early diagnosis of ADHD?

Dan's parents and teachers became concerned about his behavior when he was in grade school. His mind wandered during class—and his body did too; Dan would get up and walk around, even out of the room. "Until middle school, I couldn't understand why anyone was fussing. I just thought of myself as normal," says Dan, 14, from Fairfield, Conn. One day he realized, "Hey, other kids don't have so much [of a] problem paying attention."

## The ABCs of ADHD

Dan was showing the classic symptoms of attention-deficit/hyperactivity disorder (ADHD), according to Dr. Andrew Adesman, chief of developmental and behavioral pediatrics at Schneider Children's Hospital in New Hyde Park, N.Y. Adesman explained that ADHD is "a biological disorder characterized by significant difficulty with attention span." This isn't just doctorspeak. People with this condition really do have a hard time staying focused. To complicate matters, ADHD often teams up with impulse control problems and learning disorders. The Centers for Disease Control and Prevention estimates that 8 percent of 4- to 17-year-olds (4.4 million) are diagnosed with ADHD, and 56 percent of those are taking medication for the condition.

No one knows exactly what causes ADHD, though there may be "a genetic component," says Dr. Stephanie Hamarman, chief of psychiatry at the Stanley S. Lamm Institute in Brooklyn, N.Y., who has been working with children with ADHD for many years. In other words, people are probably born with ADHD, and scientists think it may run in families.

However, other biological and environmental factors may be involved, Adesman explains. "The part of the brain that controls how we pay attention is delicate and susceptible to injury," he adds.

Though other genetic conditions, such as asthma, epilepsy, and diabetes, can be determined through blood tests, X-rays, or other exams, no medical test yet diagnoses ADHD. "That doesn't mean that doctors won't ever be able to use a brain scan to detect ADHD," Hamarman says. "We are discovering more about the brain and about ADHD every day."

## Diagnosing the Invisible

Most doctors diagnose ADHD by observing behavior, Dr. David W. Goodman, an ADHD specialist at the Johns Hopkins University School of Medicine in Baltimore, explains. People with ADHD have difficulty concentrating and may not be able to get organized enough to begin a task, let alone finish it. The person also may interrupt people, forget things (such as homework), and have trouble keeping track of time.

But not all people who have trouble paying attention have ADHD. Perhaps they're not getting enough sleep; perhaps there are problems in the home, and they're preoccupied. Maybe they have a hearing or a vision problem, Goodman suggests. Doctors look at the severity of the symptoms.

Unfortunately, many people with ADHD are not diagnosed and treated—which can involve medication (including stimulants and antidepressants), behavior modification or alternative treatments—because their conduct isn't really unusual. "This is especially true with girls; for some reason we don't understand, girls are less frequently hyperactive," Hamarman says. The brighter a person is, the later he or she is

## "The Story of Fidgety Philip"

ADHD [attention-deficit/hyperactivity disorder] was first described by Dr. Heinrich Hoffman in 1845. A physician who wrote books on medicine and psychiatry, Dr. Hoffman was also a poet who became interested in writing for children when he couldn't find suitable materials to read to his 3-year-old son. The result was a book of poems, complete with illustrations, about children and their characteristics. "The Story of Fidgety Philip" was an accurate description of a little boy who had attention deficit hyperactivity disorder. Yet it was not until 1902 that Sir George F. Still published a series of lectures to the Royal College of Physicians in England in which he described a group of impulsive children with significant behavioral problems, caused by a genetic dysfunction and not by poor child rearing—children who today would be easily recognized as having ADHD. Since then, several thousand scientific papers on the disorder have been published, providing information on its nature, course, causes, impairments, and treatments.

*National Institute of Mental Health,*
Attention Deficit Hyperactivity Disorder, *2004.*

likely to be diagnosed, because a very smart person can compensate for the disorder. "The child isn't paying attention, but she's still getting B's. That's pretty good, so no one worries," Goodman elaborates.

## The Teen Factor

An early diagnosis, coupled with a treatment routine, is important for several reasons, says Adesman. First, the sooner a person is treated, the more he or she will benefit from treatment. Second, teens with untreated ADHD are much more likely than others to smoke cigarettes and abuse drugs. And although teens take many risks, "those with untreated ADHD take even more risks," Goodman adds. "A big problem is that someone with undiagnosed ADHD may prompt other kids to do something really dangerous," he warns.

High school students with untreated ADHD are also three times as likely as other teens to get into car accidents and lose their licenses. They are more likely to drop out of school too. Experts agree that teens with untreated ADHD are more likely to have poor self-esteem and social problems.

The earlier ADHD treatment begins, especially medication, the more likely the person is to stick with it in high school. "High school is an especially sensitive time. The less-structured environment can be very stressful, and medication helps kids deal better with stress and other teenage issues," Adesman says.

Still, newly diagnosed teens benefit from treatment almost immediately. Gabriel from New York City was diagnosed with ADHD late—his freshman year of high school. Not having a diagnosis earlier led to serious consequences; Gabriel flunked all his courses that year. "I felt that no matter what, I couldn't do the work, and the more I fell behind, the worse it got," Gabriel, now 15, remembers. When Gabriel was diagnosed with ADHD, he began taking medication. "Now I'm more hopeful," he says. He went to summer school to make up his courses and started adopting strategies that would make it easier for him to concentrate in school. Gabriel's experience shows that even if a person's ADHD isn't identified until high school or adulthood, he or she can still immediately benefit from treatment and can function as well as others.

## Managing ADHD

One of Gabriel's strategies involves watching how good students function. "I see what they do, and I copy it," he says. In class, Gabriel turns his chair so that he's facing the board and can't be distracted by others—a practice experts recommend. They also suggest the following:

- Keep one set of books at home to always be prepared to do homework.

- Ask family for help in getting organized. A parent can remind a teen of a project's due date and help him or her work on it every day instead of at the last minute.

- Do only a little work at a time, taking a break, and then getting back to work. "If I try to do homework all at once, I'm more likely to get distracted." Dan says.

- Take advantage of coaching. Many schools have re-source rooms where smaller classes make it easier for students to pay attention.

## Doing Well With ADHD

Here's the good news: Young people who receive treatment for ADHD are just as likely to do well in school and in life as anyone else. "A patient of mine just graduated [from] college at the top of her class," Adesman says.

Still, there are things kids with ADHD wish others knew. "You don't have to talk slowly," says Gabriel. "I understand English."

Dan adds, "Teachers need to be patient, but at the same time, they need to know that if I want to be treated like everyone else, I know I have to live up to expectations."

New treatments make life easier for people with ADHD. But one of the biggest breakthroughs has been the change in attitude over the past two decades, says Adesman. For instance, studies show that teens are less likely to stigmatize ADHD than are grown-ups.

So if your class includes students with ADHD, treat them as you would want to be treated. Teens with ADHD need people to be patient and helpful. In other ways, they're just like everyone else.

## ADHD Didn't Stop Me!

Type "famous people" and "ADHD" into an internet search engine, and you'll find Web page after Web page claiming that Mozart, Einstein, and other well-known dead people had ADHD. However, there's no need to search history books to find successful people who had the disorder. The following celebrities have talked about having ADHD:

- Ellen DeGeneres, comedian and actor

- Scott Eyre, relief pitcher for the San Francisco Giants

- David Neeleman, founder and CEO of JetBlue Airways

- Philip Manuel, jazz musician

> *"For most normal kids ADHD turns out to be a questionable 'disease' at best, and a bogus disease at worst."*

# Attention-Deficit/Hyperactivity Disorder Is Not a Disease

*Joel Turtel*

*In the following viewpoint, Joel Turtel claims that attention-deficit/hyperactivity disorder (ADHD) is not a true disease. In his view, children diagnosed with ADHD are probably just bored due to inadequate public schools. He contends that ADHD symptoms might also reflect stresses outside the classroom. In fact, he says, supposed ADHD symptoms mirror the symptoms of other medical conditions such as hypoglycemia, thyroid problems, and sleeping disorders. In truth, Turtel reasons, there are no objective criteria for diagnosing ADHD. Turtel, an education policy analyst, is the author of* Public Schools, Public Menace: How Public Schools Lie to Parents and Betray Our Children.

As you read, consider the following questions:

1. In Turtel's opinion, what are some of the stresses that can produce ADHD-like symptoms?

2. According to the author, why is it impossible for any teacher, principal, or family doctor to claim with certainty that a child has ADHD?

3. What does the author claim some adults do when faced with "normal behavioral variations" that result in "dissonant environmental interactions"?

The vast majority of Ritalin and Adderall is given to school children to treat an alleged disease called ADHD (Attention Deficit Hyperactivity Disorder). Children who suffer from ADHD are said to be inattentive, impulsive, and hyperactive. They often get bored easily in class, squirm in their seats, are always on the go, or don't get along with other students or the teacher. In other words, many children diagnosed with ADHD may simply be normal kids, full of energy, and bored out of their minds sitting in mind-numbing, public-school classrooms.

## Perfectly Normal Children

In his testimony to the Pennsylvania House Democratic Policy Committee, Bruce Wiseman, National President of the Citizens Commission on Human Rights, stated that "thousands of children put on psychiatric drugs are simply 'smart.'" He quoted the late Sydney Walker, a psychiatrist and neurologist, as saying, "They're hyper not because their brains don't work right, but because they spend most of the day waiting for slower students to catch up with them. These students are bored to tears, and people who are bored fidget, wiggle, scratch, stretch, and (especially if they are boys) start looking for ways to get into trouble."

Boredom is not the only reason children can exhibit symptoms of ADHD. Perfectly normal children who are over-active (have a lot of energy), rebellious, impulsive, day-dreamers, sensitive, undisciplined, bored easily (because they are bright),

"The blood tests confirm what we thought: he has ALBD—Annoying Little Bastard Disorder." Cartoon by Andrew Exton. www.CartoonStock.com.

slow in learning, immature, troubled (for any number of reasons), learning disabled (dyslexia, for example), can also be inattentive, impulsive, or hyperactive.

Many factors outside the classroom can stress or emotionally affect children, causing some children to exhibit ADHD-like 'symptoms.' Some of these factors are: not getting love, closeness, or attention from their parents; if a parent, friend, or sibling is sick or dies; if the parents are divorcing and there is anger, shouting, or conflict at home; domestic violence at home; sexual, physical, or emotional abuse by parents or siblings; inattention and neglect at home; personality clashes with parents or siblings; envy or cruelty directed at a child by classmates or by siblings at home, and many other factors.

## Conditions That Mimic ADHD

Also, many other medical conditions can cause children to mimic some or all of ADHD's symptoms. Some of these conditions are: Hypoglycemia (low blood sugar), allergies, learning disabilities, hyper or hypothyroidism, hearing and vision problems, mild to high lead levels, spinal problems, toxin exposures, carbon monoxide poisoning, metabolic disorders, genetic defects, sleeping disorders, post-traumatic subclinical seizure disorder, high mercury levels, iron deficiency, B-vitamin deficiencies (from poor diet), Tourette's syndrome, Sensory Integration Dysfunction, early-onset diabetes, heart disease, cardiac conditions, early-onset bipolar disorder, worms, viral and bacterial infections, malnutrition or improper diet, head injuries, lack of exercise, and many others.

Because these medical conditions can cause some or all of ADIID's symptoms, it becomes next to impossible for any teacher, principal, or family doctor to claim with any certainty that a child has ADHD. To be certain, a doctor would have to test the child for all these other possible medical conditions. Since parents or doctors don't do this, every diagnosis of ADHD is suspect, to say the least.

Any of these medical conditions, normal personality variations, emotional problems, or outside-the-classroom stress-factors can disturb a child's attention, natural enthusiasm, or desire to learn in class, and make the child exhibit symptoms of ADHD. Yet, as psychiatrist Peter R. Breggin, author of *Talking Back To Ritalin*, and director of the International Center for the Study of Psychiatry and Psychology, notes, "These are the types of children who get diagnosed as suffering ADHD and who get subdued with stimulants and other medications."

## Experts Deny the Existence of ADHD

Many reputable authorities deny that ADHD, the disorder for which Ritalin is most commonly prescribed, even exists. According to Breggin in *Talking Back To Ritalin*:

> There are no objective diagnostic criteria for ADHD . . . no physical symptoms, no neurological signs, and no blood tests. ADHD and Ritalin are American and Canadian medical fads. The U.S. uses 90% of the world's Ritalin . . . there is no solid evidence that ADHD is a genuine disorder or disease of any kind . . . there is no proof of any physical abnormalities in the brains or bodies of children who are routinely labeled ADHD. They do not have known biochemical imbalances or 'crossed wires' . . . ADHD is a controversial diagnosis with little or no scientific basis . . . A parent, teacher, or doctor can feel in good company when utterly dismissing the diagnosis and refusing to apply it to children.

Many other medical professionals agree with Dr. Breggin. William Carey, a professor of pediatrics at the University of Pennsylvania concluded that:

"The behaviors associated with ADHD diagnosis reflect a continuum or spectrum of normal temperaments rather than a disorder." He declared that, "ADHD appears to be a set of normal behavioral variations" that lead to "dissonant environmental interactions." That is, when the varied but normal temperaments of children bring them into conflict with parents and teachers, the adults try to end the conflicts by diagnosing the children with ADHD.

## Blaming the Victim

In other words, by labeling these normal personality traits of children a "disease," public school authorities in many states can now pressure parents to give their children mind-altering drugs to make the kids "behave" in class. This is a classic case of blaming the victim, the children, for public schools' education deficit disorder.

Parents, do not fall for the ADHD arguments that some public school authorities are now attempting to foist on you and your children. Although a few children do exhibit extreme "symptoms" of ADHD, for most normal kids ADHD turns out to be a questionable "disease" at best, and a bogus disease at worst. Many public schools now use this alleged ADHD disease as a convenient excuse to pressure parents to give their normal but bored or high-energy children mind-altering drugs. . . .

Parents, do not succumb to the temptation to drug your children with mind-altering drugs because a public-school teacher or school nurse tells you that your child is not "behaving properly" or "paying attention" in class. There are many other ways to deal with children's "behavior" problems in school besides drugging your children. One of the best ways is to *take your children out of public school so they aren't bored to death sitting in public school classrooms*. When children get engrossed in learning in a stimulating homeschool environment, they are far less likely to misbehave.

> *"Because of ADD, my life has been a roller coaster of successes and disappointments in all walks of life."*

# Adults with Attention-Deficit/ Hyperactivity Disorder Face Serious Challenges

*John Wanner*

*Adults who suffer from attention deficit disorder (ADD) often live a life of extreme highs and lows, maintains John Wanner in the following viewpoint. They struggle in traditional colleges that require prolonged study, he asserts, and because adults with ADD are bored easily, they often move from job to job. According to Wanner, they may also have troubled relationships, often blaming others for their problems. However, those clinically diagnosed with ADD have a better chance of understanding their behavior and finding ways to adapt. Wanner is an Employee Assistance Program consultant who suffers from ADD.*

As you read, consider the following questions:

1. According to Wanner, on what population has the emphasis on ADD been directed?

John Wanner, "Addressing Attention Deficit Disorder in Adults," *The Journal of Employee Assistance*, vol. 37, October 2007, pp. 27–28. Copyright © 2007 Employee Assistance Professionals. Reproduced by permission.

2. What trait has plagued the author throughout his scholastic and professional careers?

3. How does the author describe his varied college experiences?

The emphasis on ADD [attention deficit disorder] has long been on children, especially boys. Not until my daughter was diagnosed with attention deficit hyperactivity disorder [ADHD] and successfully treated did I begin to question my own attention deficit symptoms, which had begun to surface when I started school.

Like most people with ADD, I had problems in school. I flunked or barely passed many classes at all levels—from elementary school to college. If I were in school today with my symptoms, I would be diagnosed with ADHD. But in the 1950s and 1960s, ADHD was unknown.

ADD people have a hard time with processes and prolonged studying. They get bored easily and find it difficult to concentrate; they like quick fixes and short reading assignments. I myself am readily distracted, and this trait has plagued me throughout my scholastic and professional careers (I have had 20—yes, 20—jobs since college).

Like many people with ADD, I also have experienced relationship problems, used illicit substances, and confronted anger and grief issues (many due to low self-esteem). But I always blamed others—people with ADD typically blame others instead of looking at themselves.

## A Roller Coaster Existence

Because of ADD, my life has been a roller coaster of successes and disappointments in all walks of life. I flunked out of preveterinary school after 3 years of horrible grades, then returned to college, took courses in social sciences, and earned a "B-plus" average (I graduated from a small Catholic college where the nuns had time to coach me with difficult subjects, like statistics and sociological theory). I later enrolled in a weekend master's program in community development, which eventually led to my career in mental health services.

In 1964 I married my first wife, but we divorced after 12 years when money became tight. I had gone into alcohol counseling, but I grew bored staying in an office all day and doing paperwork. I accepted another position as a regional criminal justice coordinator, but soon got fired. I then discovered sales—I had taken the Myers-Briggs test [a widely used personality test, sometimes used in vocational settings], which showed I was perfect for sales work—but my pay wasn't steady, as I was on commission.

After the divorce, I moved to an apartment and started smoking marijuana. I finally landed another sales job selling food plans to homeowners. I won numerous sales awards for my efforts and doubled my previous income. Everything seemed perfect—I was closing sales quickly, filing minimal paperwork, and getting high while I worked.

My employer then sent me to open a new office in Kentucky. By this time I had met a woman in my apartment building and we had started dating. We moved to Kentucky and got married, I started making sales, and my son (from my first marriage) found new friends.

Then the economy slowed, causing my customers' financing to dry up. My wife and I were desperate for money and decided to move to Florida and live with my parents.

I soon landed a job evaluating drunk drivers. I was appointed assistant director after two years, but I started to get bored and had anger problems with my son and occasionally with clients. Then, disaster struck—my wife suffered a fatal heart attack in July 1987.

Through a "friend/angel," my boss learned I was smoking pot. I was given a choice: use the EAP [employee assistance program] (which offered inpatient treatment) or be fired. I surrendered and checked myself into drug treatment.

## The Adult with ADHD

Not unlike some children with ADHD [attention-deficit/ hyperactivity disorder], adults with ADHD tend to have "executive function" defects, which include organizational problems as well as difficulties with problem solving. Adults with ADHD tend to have difficulties with educational achievement and do best if their curriculum is structured. Academic problems continue to manifest themselves as underachievement in college. Frequently, there is a history of suspension of driver's licenses for DUI [driving under the influence of alcohol or drugs] and other violations.

*Nedd Rapp,*
*"Attention Deficit Hyperactivity Disorder in Adults:*
*Review of an Article,"* The Exceptional Parent,
*September 2007.*

After 45 days I was discharged and went back to work. I attended 12-step meetings and grief counseling sessions. But to maintain my sobriety, I needed to change jobs.

I took a couple of other counseling positions, but I still had trouble focusing and staying on task. I was told it was "brain fog" from the marijuana leaving the brain, or just a part of the detox process. I thought, "I've been sober for a year and I'm still having the same problems I had before treatment. Why is this happening to me?"

In 1991 I married a sweet woman, Laurel, and we moved to North Carolina. I accepted a position as an EAP assistant coordinator for a local mental health center and was promoted to director the next year. Three years later I began a long relationship with a private EAP selling EA programs, seeing clients, and conducting wellness programs.

Though my life had improved, my ADD hadn't gone away. I was still negative, had anxiety problems, and wasn't truly at peace.

## Relieved and Disappointed

By this time, Laurel and I had decided to adopt a child. After a nine-month wait we met our daughter, Alita, in Guatemala, on Dec. 4, 1999, her first birthday. She is a true joy in our life.

When Alita entered pre-school, she started having some learning difficulties and experiencing other behavioral problems. We had her tested and found she had a learning disability and ADHD.

In 2003 we moved to South Carolina because my wife was transferred. The hospital where she worked had an EAP which we utilized for Alita's treatment. After months of using various medications and receiving counseling, Alita was successful with neurofeedback, an alternative treatment in which sensors are placed on the head to measure brain wave activity while the patient watches and/or controls a video game. She stopped taking psychotropic medications and receiving counseling, and is doing very well.

Laurel suggested that I make an appointment to see an EA professional, since I exhibited many of Alita's ADHD symptoms. I was tested for, and diagnosed with, adult ADD.

I was both relieved and disappointed—relieved that after 62 years I had finally learned why I thought the way I thought and did the things I did, and disappointed that I hadn't been diagnosed sooner. I've come to accept that I can't change my past, but I want to help change the future for other adults with ADD.

*"My ADHD has helped me as a scholar much more than it has impeded me."*

# Adult Attention-Deficit/ Hyperactivity Disorder Is a Gift, Not a Disease

*Sarah Rasher*

*In the following viewpoint, Sarah Rasher relates how her adult attention-deficit/hyperactivity disorder (ADHD) has been more of a help than a hindrance. As a child, she had trouble sitting still and paying attention and would erupt when frustrated. However, by high school she had learned to mask her feelings. Those with ADHD, she argues, are multitaskers and think beyond traditional concepts, coming up with creative new ideas. According to Rasher, these skills have made her a better scholar and teacher. Rasher is working toward her PhD in English literature at the University of Connecticut.*

As you read, consider the following questions:

1. In Rasher's opinion, what has been one unfortunate outcome of learning to control her emotions?

Sarah Rasher, "Disorderly Conduct," *The Chronicle of Higher Education*, vol. 55, October 10, 2008, p. B24. Copyright © 2008 by The Chronicle of Higher Education. Reproduced by permission of the author.

2. According to the author, under what circumstances would she need to go through psychological tests?

3. In the author's view, what does teaching give her an excuse to be?

When I was 5, my Hebrew-school teacher told my mom that I was mentally disabled. I did indeed have difficulty following instructions, and I fidgeted during story time. There had already been a brief scandal in preschool because I interpreted "sharing is caring" as a plot to brainwash me into giving up my toys and interacting with kids I didn't like. At about the same time, I had been expelled from ballet school for leaving the line of tiny ballerinas to break into a costume closet and try on all the hats. My mother knew I was trouble.

"My daughter figured out how to read when she was 3 years old," my mom explained to the Hebrew-school teacher. "Have you ever considered that she's bored?"

All the other kids loved filmstrips and the story rug, the rare opportunities to absorb information passively. But I would squirm the whole time, tapping out rhythms on the floor with my toes, filling loose-leaf paper with intricate abstract doodles. I would look around the room at the rapt faces of my classmates, wondering how they could pay attention to one thing for so long. By fifth grade, I was doing prealgebra and reading at a college level. I'd figured out the byzantine social rules of primary school and had a steady group of friends. But all the other kids seemed to have mastered something I couldn't fathom—sitting still and paying attention.

## Learning to Cope

By high school, I'd learned how to mask my problem. Until then, there had been only one trait that had stood out; when frustrated, I would erupt into uncontrollable outbursts of crying. With the help of a school psychologist and then therapy, I learned to control my emotions, to the point where I am now considered cold and heartless.

I also discovered, in high school, the medicinal effects of caffeine, which paradoxically reduced my nervous energy. Most of all, I overextended myself: If I was so busy that I had to do my Spanish homework in homeroom, my math homework in Spanish class, and my poem for the writing club in math class, I wouldn't have time for boredom. If I didn't have time to sit still, no one would notice that I literally could not sit still.

My well-developed coping mechanisms helped me succeed in high school. But I was tired of working the system, so I attended a college more suited to my temperament. At Sarah Lawrence, nearly all of my courses were limited to 15 students, and half of our work was independent study. Instead of being publicly humiliated in English class for my anti-authoritarian interpretation of *Julius Caesar*, I was recommended for a year of studying Shakespeare at the University of Oxford. Instead of writing poetry in honors precalculus and then meeting with the teacher after school so he could explain the day's lesson to me in terms other than rote memorization, I was writing a paper applying principles of game theory to *The Importance of Being Earnest*. I was supposed to talk in class, to devote late nights to reading about strange things that fascinated me, to think the way I actually thought.

## A Moment of Clarity

I thrived in college, but my sophomore year brought crises. I was co-directing a difficult comedy show; I'd broken up with my first real girlfriend; my grandmother was dying of colon cancer. Two problem sets behind in calculus, I broke down crying during an independent-study meeting with my math professor, who suggested I go to student counseling. I went and was relieved to hear that I wasn't handling my situation too badly—the first time I'd heard such a thing from a school counselor. But I needed to get those problem sets done, so we talked about academics. The counselor dragged my history

## A New Hero, a New Debate

When pediatricians diagnose attention deficit hyperactivity disorder, they often ask their patients whether they know anybody else with the problem.

These days, children are likely to reply with a household name: Michael Phelps. . . .

But the emergence of a major celebrity with attention deficit has revealed a schism in the community of patients, parents, doctors and educators who deal with the disorder. For years, these people have debated whether it means a lifetime of limitations or whether it can sometimes be a good thing.

*Tara Parker-Pope,*
*"A New Face for A.D.H.D., and a Debate,"*
New York Times, *November 25, 2008.*

out of me: the fidgeting, the caffeine addiction, the emotional outbursts. She asked me follow-up questions. Did I find it hard to study in the library? Did I think better if I was moving around? Did I often notice movements or noises that other people seemed to be ignoring?

How did she know me so well?

She asked if I had ever been tested for ADHD—attention-deficit hyperactivity disorder. I had not. She told me that she wasn't qualified to offer a clinical diagnosis but that I'd aced the quiz. I feared being put through psychological tests at such a fragile point in my life, and the counselor told me I'd only need to do so if I wanted to go on medication or receive learning-disability services. We agreed that I didn't need those things, as my assignments were delayed by grief and over-scheduling, not by ADHD. What I'd really needed was someone to talk to. I did my problem sets; I delegated some of the production tasks for the show; I notified my professors of my family situation and set aside time to grieve.

## Personality Traits, Not Symptoms

I've never gotten around to that psychiatrist's appointment because I don't really want to be treated. I was almost 20 years old when I met with that counselor, and by then my "symptoms" were more like personality traits. Some of my coping skills are less than ideal, but I think their side effects are milder than those of medication. It's hard to think of something as a condition, a disorder, or a disability when for most of my life it's just been me.

As I've moved into my late 20s, I've solidified what it means to be an adult with ADHD. In graduate school, I've disclosed it to professors when appropriate, mostly warning them not to be offended if I doodle or bounce in my seat. In most cases, it's the first time they've heard such a confession from a grad student. Some psychiatric conditions, like clinical depression, suit the stereotype of Ph.D. candidates in English, but ADHD carries the opposite kind of connotation. As a culture, we assume that people with ADHD are anti-intellectual jocks—the ones who beat up future academics, not the future academics themselves.

But aside from occasionally irritating my colleagues when I tap my feet during conference presentations, my ADHD has helped me as a scholar much more than it has impeded me. People with ADHD are natural multitaskers; our wandering minds make conceptual connections that others miss. ADHD minds don't just color outside the lines—they get crayon all over the furniture. In academe we call that intertextuality, intersectionality, interdisciplinarity. In high school, I was scolded for making bold connections; as a Ph.D. candidate, I am told that this is what will get me published.

## Teaching as Therapy

[In 2007] I had a student who hung around after the first day of class to tell me he had ADHD. He told me he was pretty sure he wouldn't need any special accommodations in my class, because it seemed ADHD-friendly. "I do my best," I said with a lump in my throat I had not felt since coming out as bisexual in high school. "I have it, too." When he came to the one-on-one meetings that were a component of the course, we marveled at the similarity of our experiences. Because he was male and younger than me, he'd been treated for the disorder more aggressively, and he was proud to have kicked Ritalin before starting college. But the squirming, the reading and daydreaming and getting in trouble, the love for learning almost squashed by teachers who didn't know what to do with us—we had the same story. He was in the process of changing his major to secondary education, and we found that we were drawn to teaching for the same reasons. Teaching is an outlet for and an antidote to restlessness, an excuse to be mobile and noisy. But more important, we'd been through education hell, and we wanted to protect others from it.

[In 2008] I found out that I'd won my department's teaching award for graduate students. I used to joke that my only real goal in teaching was to keep students from getting as bored as I used to get, but I think it works both ways: They know they're not allowed to bore me, either.

The simple goal of staying engaged may not compensate for all or even most cases of ADHD, but it seems to work for me and for my students. It's not just the fidgety kids who want a reason to sit still.

> "*[By 2001] the rates for kids with autism had exploded. Suddenly, doctors and educators knew about autism. Kids with autism were everywhere.*"

# Autism Is a Serious Public Health Crisis

*Anne McElroy Dachel*

*In the following viewpoint, Anne McElroy Dachel notes that the number of children with autism has skyrocketed since the late 1980s. She maintains that this increase coincides with a corresponding increase in the number of mercury-containing vaccines recommended by the Centers for Disease Control and Prevention (CDC), but the CDC denies any connection. The CDC has produced studies to back up what Dachel calls "the really big lie"—that autism is not an epidemic, she claims. However, when vast numbers of autistic children begin to require costly services, Dachel reasons, the lie will no longer hold up. Dachel is the mother of an autistic son.*

Anne McElroy Dachel, "The Really Big Lie About Autism," YubaNet.com, August 22, 2006. Copyright © 2007 YubaNet.com. Reproduced by permission.

As you read, consider the following questions:

1. In Dachel's opinion, what did the CDC not think to do when they mandated new vaccines?

2. When did the author first hear of the autism gene?

3. What sign does the author believe indicates we are fast approaching a crisis that will expose "the really big lie"?

This commentary is about something I've come to call, "the really big lie," which is surely based on the theory that the masses are more willing to believe totally illogical, absurd propaganda, than a small little lie.

I'm talking about the claim by the medical community, health officials, educators, and a vast parade of reporters, that the epidemic in kids with autism and related disorders overwhelming our schools, is the result of "greater awareness" and "better diagnosing."

I've been living with the really big lie for years but by now I am totally dumbstruck by the fact that it's still believed. It's not a lie as far as everyone who repeats it. To be fair, while it's a lie for many, it's a fallacy, medical myth, or just wishful thinking for others.

## Rationalizing a Health Care Disaster

It's a crazy way to rationalize a health care disaster, but it works! I see it every day in the press, usually backed up by quotes from a CDC [Centers for Disease Control and Prevention] official or a doctor. I've rarely, if ever, heard anyone in the mainstream media challenge people who make this pronouncement.

I'm constantly pointing out that the explosion in special needs kids in our school can't be explained away so simply, but no one seems to notice.

Although I have no proof of my belief, I'm inclined to think that the really big lie was started by some nameless individual deep within the recesses of the Centers for Disease Control and Prevention in Atlanta, being CDC officials never seem to tire of repeating the really big lie.

When faced with the skyrocketing increase in autism from one in 10,000 children, to one in every 166, including one in every 80 males, in just twenty years, coupled with the knowledge that this happened at the very same time that the CDC dramatically increased the number of mercury-containing vaccines on the childhood immunization schedule, CDC officials had to be desperate.

They never thought to add up the cumulative mercury totals with each new shot on the schedule and they had mandated each vaccine. The blame would fall squarely on their shoulders.

The CDC's response has been complete denial; after all if there was no real increase in disorders, everyone would be off the hook.

Thus was born the really big lie: There really aren't more children with autism. They've always been out there, we just didn't identify the problem as autism.

Like with all big lies, there must be proof to back it up and the CDC has given us lots of experts, studies, and findings of their own to do just that. I can't imagine the CDC getting away with the really big lie if it were used in attempt to explain away an epidemic of any disease affecting children, but because of the varied symptoms of the autism spectrum disorders, it seems to have worked for autism.

## Living with the Lie

Since my son is almost 20, I've lived with the really big lie almost since its inception. In fact, I was probably among the first to hear it. This gives me a unique perspective and likely caused me to be a bit more skeptical about the really big lie than most people.

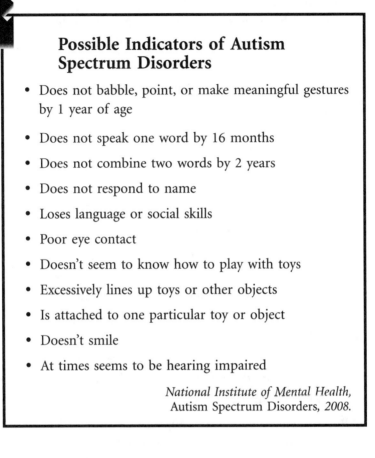

## Possible Indicators of Autism Spectrum Disorders

- Does not babble, point, or make meaningful gestures by 1 year of age

- Does not speak one word by 16 months

- Does not combine two words by 2 years

- Does not respond to name

- Loses language or social skills

- Poor eye contact

- Doesn't seem to know how to play with toys

- Excessively lines up toys or other objects

- Is attached to one particular toy or object

- Doesn't smile

- At times seems to be hearing impaired

*National Institute of Mental Health,*
Autism Spectrum Disorders, *2008.*

When John was three, his talking and interacting with people began to regress. It was so subtle that it's hard to remember when he first wasn't the alert, energetic little toddler he once was. Nobody seemed all that alarmed about it but me.

I enrolled him in a speech therapy class at the university which helped a little, but no one could explain why this was happening. I enrolled John in school at five and the next four years were one long struggle that I'd like to not even think about. No one understood him and his autistic behaviors were viewed as signs of immaturity, defiance, and anxiety.

In the second grade in 1993, John was diagnosed as "possibly autistic" by a psychologist from Minneapolis. I'll never forget how she made the statement that autism was a "rare disorder."

She said that it was doubtful that John would ever be able to live independently or hold a job. It was all rather hopeless and I was left pretty much on my own when it came to finding information on autism. So much was said back then about the rareness of the disorder.

## Coping with the Problem Alone

We live in a town of 14,000 people and when I read that the autism rate was one in 10,000, I figured that it was unlikely that I would ever find another parent with an autistic child.

Although I taught school for eight years before I was married, I had never heard of a student with autism. This of course was all in the days before the invention of the really big lie, when the truth was still discussed about autism affecting only a small number of kids.

After what seemed a very long stay in grade school, where no professionals had any training or experience with handling kids with autism, starting in the fourth grade, I home schooled John.

Those were the good years. He learned at his own pace. Being a teacher myself, I designed a curriculum that he could work with. Some things he could do with no help, others were like a hopeless mystery.

John took piano, and we were all in 4-H [a youth organization that targets four areas of personal development: head, heart, hands, and health] and belonged to a home school social group. We took vacations and John had a paper route, but he was still pretty unresponsive when he was around strangers and he didn't like to go to public places.

When John was fifteen, everything changed. I found a doctor who specialized in developmental disorders. I wanted to learn how to get John to interact more with people.

## An Explosion of Autism

This was when I got the shock of my life. In the eight years since John's original diagnosis at seven-years-old, the rates for kids with autism had exploded. Suddenly, doctors and educators knew about autism. Kids with autism were everywhere. The doctor's assistant even had two autistic sons of her own.

In fact, I learned that now there was a whole spectrum of autistic disorders and John's was called Asperger's Syndrome.

I'm pretty sure that this was when I was told the really big lie for the first time—that all of the autistic kids were the result of "greater awareness and better diagnosing," and that autistic children used to just "fall through the cracks" or were labeled with other disorders.

It didn't make much sense, but at least I had a lot of company now.

John's doctor had us combing through our family tree trying to find our "autistic relatives" that were labeled with something besides autism. This was also when I first heard of the "autism gene" supposedly responsible for this "inherited condition."

When I was first told that John had Asperger's Syndrome it was such a rush of relief because I assumed that there would be people to help John and school programs for kids like John that were not available when he was diagnosed eight years earlier.

This is when I realized that the really big lie was just that, a really big lie. There was a huge disconnect between the really big lie and the reality of services. If these kids had been always been around, what had the schools done with them?

I mean, it's impossible to ignore a child with autism, they must have had something for them. I was one of the original members of an Asperger's Syndrome parent group at a local hospital and I met so many people just like me struggling with children and nowhere to turn to.

When I first started hearing about the rise in autism cases, I knew immediately that John and others like him were just the tip of a very large iceberg hidden underwater for the moment but not for long.

The one thing that scares me more than anything else in life is wondering what will happen to these kids once they are adults if we can't even provide for them in schools as kids.

My son is considered mildly affected with autism now. He is much improved from the hopeless student in the second grade. He is fabulous on a computer, he has his driver's license, he rides horseback and plays the organ and piano. He is great at conversation at home now, but his social skills are still limited in new situations and with strangers.

## An Aging Autistic Population

Once he finished school, John became eligible for Social Security disability payments. When my husband took John to apply, the Social Security worker filling out the forms asked, "Why are there all these young people with autism going on disability?"

Evidently, she hadn't yet heard the really big lie, being she was so surprised at all the people with autism. My husband told her to get used to it, there were lots more coming, including many who were severely disabled in need of much more help than John.

The reaction of the young Social Security worker could be a sign that we're fast approaching a crisis with the really big lie that threatens to expose it to all.

Right now, eighty percent of autistic Americans are under the age of 18. This is another thing nobody seems to think about. What happens when one out of every 166 eighteen-year-olds goes on disability for life with autism?

Years ago, I used to hear projections about the enormous cost to society when the baby boomer generation retired. I don't hear anything about the generation with autism. They won't have pension plans, IRA's [individual retirement accounts], veteran's benefits, or home equity. They will never pay into Social Security, but they will need to live on disability payments for life.

I don't know how much longer the really big lie is going to work. Throughout history, there have been many plagues and diseases that have resulted in the deaths of millions, but this will be the first time a society has been left with a generation of disabled young people to care for.

When the American taxpayers realize that their bill for all this "greater awareness and better diagnosing" will be in the trillions, I don't think they're going to buy the really big lie.

I suppose government officials will then have to invent a new lie. Only this time it will have to be a really, *really* big lie and I can hardly wait to see what they come up with.

*"The likely reasons for the increase in autism prevalence are the broadening of the diagnostic rules for the disorder, better sampling . . . and better diagnostic precision."*

# Autism Is Not an Epidemic

## Lawrence Scahill

*The rise in autism diagnoses is not an indication that autism has reached epidemic proportions, maintains Lawrence Scahill in the following viewpoint. He contends that one explanation for the rise is a broadened diagnostic definition. Moreover, Scahill argues, techniques for identifying instances of autism in the broader community have improved. Since the rise in numbers can be explained by improved diagnoses and sampling techniques, he reasons that environmental changes are not likely the cause. Scahill, a professor of nursing and child psychiatry, is the director of research on pediatric psychopharmacology at the Yale University Child Study Center.*

As you read, consider the following questions:

1. According to Scahill, what happens any time you broaden the definition of a disorder?

Lawrence Scahill, "Autism Is Not an Epidemic," *Pediatric News*, vol. 42, April 2008, p. 24. Copyright © 2008 International Medical News Group. Reproduced by permission.

2. In a 1987 to 1994 California study, what happened to the prevalence of mental retardation during the period when autism increased?

3. Why does the author argue that the autism increase is not attributable to genetics?

Clinicians who treat children who have pervasive developmental disorders are likely to be asked by parents to explain the rising prevalence of autism and the possible environmental causes. Let me offer a brief background and a few facts that may help to address these questions and show that autism is not an epidemic.

## Looking at the Numbers

Let's start with the numbers. Historically, autism was considered a rare disorder with a reported prevalence of 2–5 cases per 10,000. Today, prevalence estimates are 20 per 10,000 for autism and about 60 per 10,000 for pervasive developmental disorders. This is not a trivial difference, but I do not believe that the change represents a rise in new cases—a requirement for an epidemic.

The likely reasons for the increase in autism prevalence are the broadening of the diagnostic rules for the disorder, better sampling of cases in the community, and better diagnostic precision.

Let's look first at classification. In 1994, DSM-IV [*Diagnostic and Statistical Manual of Mental Disorders*, fourth edition, a comprehensive classification of officially recognized psychiatric disorders] broadened the diagnostic definition for autism and the potentially related disorders of Asperger's disorder and pervasive disorder not otherwise specified. Any time you broaden the definition of a disorder, the prevalence of that condition will go up.

Next there's the issue of sampling. In the past, researchers estimated prevalence by counting all the known cases identi-

## A False Impression

Roy Richard Grinker, a professor of anthropology at George Washington University, argues that many factors have conspired to give the false impression of an [autism] epidemic. Psychiatrists have broadened the diagnosis of autism to include more people; society now recognizes the disorder more readily, so children are getting diagnosed more often and at younger ages; and there are more child psychiatrists who are familiar with and can diagnose the disorder.

*Richard Monastersky, "Is There an Autism Epidemic?"*
The Chronicle of Higher Education, *May 11, 2007.*

fied by clinicians in the field. In psychiatric epidemiology, this approach always resulted in an underestimate of the prevalence. There always was a gap between identified cases and all cases. This was shown for depression, attention-deficit/hyperactivity disorder, obsessive-compulsive disorder—to name a few. Even with serious disorders like autism, cases went unidentified. Newer studies surveyed the community to include previously unidentified cases in the estimate of prevalence, thus correcting the systematic undercounting of cases and providing a more accurate estimate of prevalence.

## The Challenge of Diagnostic Precision

Finally, there's the issue of diagnostic precision. In the past, the instruments were not very good at differentiating between children with mental retardation alone and those with both autism and mental retardation. Similarly, children in the average IQ range rarely were diagnosed with autism and rarely contributed to the numerator in the expression of prevalence. Today the diagnostic tools are far from perfect, but they are more precise and capable of making the diagnosis in both lower- and higher-functioning children (i.e., those with normal or near-normal IQs).

Data from California consistently show that lower- and higher-functioning children are contributing to the rise in newly identified cases. Researchers from the March of Dimes Birth Defects Foundation and the California Department of Health Services conducted a population-based study of birth cohorts from 1987 to 1994. They found that during the study period the prevalence of autism increased from 5.8 to 14.9 per 10,000. The figures also show that during the same time period the prevalence of mental retardation decreased from 28.8 to 19.5 per 10,000.

Obviously, there were children previously classified as mentally retarded who are now being labeled as having an autism spectrum disorder. The study also showed that children in the average range of IQ were an even larger source of new cases.

## Unlikely Explanations

Now that I have made the case against an epidemic in autism, let's consider some of the unlikely explanations for the increased prevalence of autism. It would be very difficult to argue that there is a genetic explanation for the apparent rise in prevalence. The threefold increase in California, for example, is simply too rapid a rise in a single decade to be attributable to genetics. Therefore, most of the focus has been on environmental exposures such as the measles, mumps, rubella (MMR) vaccine and the use of thimerosal as a preservative in other vaccines.

The MMR vaccine has been carefully evaluated in more than one country and a causal link to autism cannot be made. Thimerosal also is an unlikely explanation. The Institute of Medicine evaluated both published and unpublished epidemiological studies in a 2004 report and found that the evidence did not support a link between the preservative and autism.

In conclusion, implied in the perceived autism epidemic is an environmental cause. However, the environmental causes do not stand up to careful scrutiny and the "epidemic" can be otherwise explained.

Although there is no epidemic, autism, Asperger's disorder, and pervasive developmental disorder not otherwise specified are more common than previously believed and are an important public health issue.

# Periodical Bibliography

*The following articles have been selected to supplement the diverse views presented in this chapter.*

Michael Agger — "Shyness: How Normal Behavior Became a Sickness," *Mother Jones*, November-December 2007.

Marc Bousquet — "Brainstorm: Oppositional and Defiant—Or Critical Thinker?" *The Chronicle Review*, September 12, 2008.

*Current Science* — "Autism Epidemic a Myth," March 28, 2008.

Charles Davenport — "ADHD Myth Mostly Based on Nonsense," *News Record* (Piedmont, NC), October 5, 2008.

Scott O. Lilienfeld and Hal Arkowitz — "Is There Really an Autism Epidemic?" *Scientific American*, December 6, 2007.

Richard Monastersky — "Is There an Autism Epidemic?" *Chronicle of Higher Education*, May 11, 2007.

Tara Parker-Pope — "A New Face for A.D.H.D., and a Debate," *New York Times*, November 25, 2008.

Nedd Rapp — "Attention Deficit Hyperactivity Disorder in Adults," *The Exceptional Parent*, September 2007.

David Safir — "Hype Around Autism," *USA Today*, February 15, 2007.

Thomas Szasz — "The Medicalization of Everyday Life," *Freeman*, December 2007.

Penny Wakefield — "PTSD: Doubly Disabling for Female Vets," *Human Rights*, Spring 2008.

OPPOSING
VIEWPOINTS®
SERIES

CHAPTER 2

# What Factors Contribute to Behavioral Disorders?

# Chapter Preface

In the eyes of many, no subject is as contentious in the behavioral disorder debate as the causes of these disorders. In
fact, despite volumes of research in recent years, whether these
disorders have organic, genetic, social, or environmental origins remains fiercely contested. While a suggested and viru-
lently contested cause of autism involves a link to vaccines,
some researchers continue to look for other causes, including
early exposure to television.

Early researchers such as Bruno Bettelheim believed that
autism was a form of psychotic behavior. He blamed cold, dis-
tant, "refrigerator" mothers. Since the cause was believed to be
poor early childhood parenting, Freudian psychoanalysis
formed the basis of therapy for autistic children. However, it
produced poor results. "There was no empirical literature
from psychodynamic interventions showing real change in
people with autism," argues Sally J. Rogers, a professor of psychiatry at the Medical Investigation of Neurodevelopmental
Disorders (MIND) Institute at the University of California at
Davis. In fact, long-standing adherence to these now discred-
ited claims made many parents suspicious of mainstream science. The belief that parents were to blame, claims autistic
parent and activist Rick Rollens, "retarded a serious effort by
science to find a real cause and proved how wrong mainstream science can be."

Once researchers stopped blaming mothers for their
children's autism, the quest to find other environmental causes
began. One study, conducted at Cornell University in Ithaca,
New York, suggests that early television viewing may be to
blame. The study found a correlation between the rising number of children diagnosed with autism in recent decades and
the increasing percentage of households with cable television.
The study also notes that among the Amish, who do not use

electricity and therefore do not watch television, autism is rare. Moreover, the study maintains, autism diagnosis rates also increase during periods of poor weather—periods in which children watch more television. The Cornell researchers explain that during a child's early years, it must engage all of its senses to develop to its full potential. The best way to do this is by interacting with the world around it—touching, tasting, and smelling. Television, these analysts reason, is a passive experience, which would therefore explain the correlation with autism. Professor Michael Waldman, who led the study, suggests that parents seriously consider the results of this study before they put children under three in front of the television.

Critics contend that the conclusions drawn by the Cornell study are unwarranted. Too many other factors could explain the results, they assert. For example, during periods of poor weather, something in the home environment other than television could explain the rise in autism. They maintain that indoor air quality is often worse than outdoor air quality. Other study opponents argue that environmental causes have little to do with autism. According to Craig Newschaffer, a researcher at Drexel University in Philadelphia, there is "a reasonable body of evidence that [suggests] that the pathologic process behind autism probably starts in utero." Indeed, a MIND study found that 95 percent of a small group of children later diagnosed as autistic had elevated levels of neuropeptides and neurotropins at birth.

For many, the quest to identify autism's causes has truly been a bitter journey. The personal experience of anguished parents, once blamed for their children's disease, are often trumped by mainstream science. Nevertheless, they continue to persevere in search of answers. This search to understand autism's causes is reflective of the search for the causes of other behavioral disorders. The voices of parents, victims, physicians, and researchers are found among the viewpoints in the following chapter, as they explore the factors that contribute to behavioral disorders.

> *"The study found boys with ADHD had significant shape differences and decreases in overall volume of the basal ganglia compared to their typically developing peers."*

# Attention-Deficit/ Hyperactivity Disorder Has Biological Causes

*NewsRx Health*

*Attention-Deficit/Hyperactivity Disorder (ADHD) has biological causes, argues NewsRx Health's editors in the following viewpoint. This claim is illustrated by a study that revealed shape differences in the brains of children with ADHD when compared with the brains of typically developing peers. The new analysis tool, large deformation diffeomorphic mapping (LDDMM), that helped researchers discover these shape differences may be the key to further research to unlock the biological causes of ADHD and improve diagnosis and treatment of patients.*

As you read, consider the following questions:

1. Did girls with ADHD have shape or volume differences when compared with their typically developing peers?

2. How old were the children used in the study, and how many children were used in the control group?

3. What are the potential next steps for research based on the findings of this study?

A study published in the online advance edition of the *American Journal of Psychiatry* for the first time reveals shape differences in the brains of children with ADHD, which could help pinpoint the specific neural circuits involved in the disorder. Researchers from the Kennedy Krieger Institute in Baltimore, Md. and the Johns Hopkins Center for Imaging Science used a new analysis tool, large deformation diffeomorphic mapping (LDDMM), which allowed them to examine the precise shape of the basal ganglia. The study found boys with ADHD had significant shape differences and decreases in overall volume of the basal ganglia compared to their typically developing peers. Girls with ADHD did not have volume or shape differences, suggesting sex strongly influences the disorder's expression.

Previous studies examining the basal ganglia in children with ADHD were limited to volume analysis and had conflicting results, with some reporting a smaller volume and some reporting no difference in volume. LDDMM provides detailed analysis of the shape of specific brain regions, allowing for precise examination of brain structures well beyond what has been examined in previous MRI studies of ADHD. In this study, LDDMM was used to map the brains of typically developing children in order to generate a basal ganglia template. This is the first reported template of the basal ganglia. After

---

**Factors That Do Not Cause ADHD**

- too much TV

- food allergies

- excess sugar

- poor home life

- poor schools

*Attention Deficit Disorder Association, "What Causes AD/HD?"*

---

creating LDDMM mappings of the basal ganglia of each child with ADHD, statistical analysis was conducted to compare them to the template.

## Specific Findings of the Study

In this study, the initial volume analysis revealed boys with ADHD had significantly smaller basal ganglia volumes compared with typically-developing boys. Moving beyond the standard volume analysis, the LDDMM revealed shape abnormalities in several regions of the basal ganglia. Comparison of the standard volume and LDDMM analysis of girls with ADHD and their typically developing peers failed to reveal any significant volume or shape differences.

The multiple shape differences found in boys with ADHD suggests that the disorder may not be associated with abnormalities in one specific neural circuit. Rather, it appears the disorder involves abnormalities in parallel circuits, including circuits important for the control of complex behavior and more basic motor responses, such as hitting the brake pedal when a traffic light turns yellow. Findings revealing abnormalities in circuits important for basic motor response control may be crucial to understanding why children with ADHD have difficulty suppressing impulsive actions.

"This study represents a major advancement in our ability to examine the neuroanatomic features of ADHD and other developmental disorders," said Dr. Stewart H. Mostofsky, senior study author and a pediatric neurologist in the Department of Developmental Cognitive Neurology at the Kennedy Krieger Institute. "Using LDDMM, we can more accurately measure the impact of ADHD on brain development, which will not only bring us closer to unlocking the biological basis of the disorder, but help us better diagnose and treat patients."

Researchers used MRI scans to examine children ages 8–13 years, including: 47 children with ADHD and a control group of 66 typically developing children. Researchers compared the LDDMM mappings of children with ADHD to their typically developing peers, and then went a step further by repeating the analysis separately for boys and girls. Children with ADHD who had a history of other neuropsychiatric diagnoses including conduct disorder, mood disorder, generalized anxiety disorder, separation anxiety disorder and/or obsessive-compulsive disorder were excluded from the study. Additionally, none of the children with ADHD had a learning disability or a history of speech/language disorders.

Potential next steps include research that carefully examines whether the brain abnormalities found in this study can predict certain behavioral features of ADHD. Future studies will also examine structural features associated with the ability to compensate and respond to therapy. The researchers also plan to use LDDMM analysis on children in a wider age range to see if changes in the basal ganglia occur over time.

*"Nowhere in the brains or bodies of children said to have ADHD or any other psychiatric diagnosis has a disorder/ disease been confirmed."*

# Attention-Deficit/ Hyperactivity Disorder Is Not a Biological Disease

*Fred Baughman*

*A disorder is a disease only if it is an objective abnormality, argues Fred Baughman in the following viewpoint. However, there is no evidence that attention-deficit/hyperactivity disorder (ADHD) is a disease, he claims. Nor is it a chemical imbalance requiring a pharmacological remedy. In his view, brain atrophy in studies of subjects with ADHD is likely the result of the subject's drug therapy. Thus, he reasons, claims that medications normalize brain function are a lie promoted by pharmaceutical companies.* Baughman is a retired neurologist and the author of The ADHD Fraud—How Psychiatry Makes "Patients" of Normal Children.

Fred Baughman, "There Is No Such Things As a Psychiatric Disorder/Disease/Chemical Imbalance," *PLoS Medicine*, vol. 3, July 2006, pp. 1189–1190. Copyright © 2006 Fred Baughman. Reproduced by permission.

As you read, consider the following questions:

1. According to Baughman, why is glue ear a disease while dyslexia is not?

2. What subjects did J. Swanson confess he and F.X. Castellanos failed to look at when studying ADHD and brain atrophy?

3. Why does the author claim that the FDA is a purveyor of the psychiatric disease and chemical imbalance lie?

In her [2006] *PLoS Medicine* article, Christine Phillips writes: "ADHD [attention-deficit/hyperactivity disorder] joins dyslexia and glue ear as disorders that are considered significant primarily because of their effects on educational performance." A "disorder" is "a disturbance of function, structure, or both," and thus, the equivalent of an objective abnormality/disease. In neurologically normal children, dyslexia cannot be proved to be a disorder/disease. "Glue ear," however, is otitis media, an objective abnormality/disease. Phillips continues: "In the case of ADHD, there has been a complex, often heated debate in the public domain about the verity of the illness," but proceeds, without an answer, to consider "the roles of teachers as brokers for ADHD and its treatment."

In 1948, "neuropsychiatry" was divided into "neurology," dealing with diseases, and "psychiatry," dealing with emotions and behaviors. If there is a macroscopic, microscopic, or chemical abnormality, a disease is present. Nowhere in the brains or bodies of children said to have ADHD or any other psychiatric diagnosis has a disorder/disease been confirmed. Psychiatric drugs appeared in the fifties. Psychiatry and the pharmaceutical industry authored the "chemical imbalance" market strategy: they would call all things psychological "chemical imbalances" needing "chemical balancers"—pills.

At the September 29, 1970, hearing on Federal Involvement in the Use of Behavior Modification Drugs on Grammar

## What Drives the Overmedication of Children?

Well-intentioned but misinformed teachers, parents using the Internet to diagnose their children, and hurried doctors are all a part of the complex system that drives the current practice of misdiagnosing and overmedicating children. The solution lies in the practice of good, conscientious medicine that is careful, thorough and patient-centered.

*Elizabeth J. Roberts,*
*"A Rush to Medicate Young Minds,"*
*Washingtonpost.com, October 8, 2006.*

School Children, Ronald Lipman of the United States Food and Drug Administration (FDA), argued: "hyperkinesis is a medical syndrome. It should be properly diagnosed by a medical doctor."

## Explaining Brain Atrophy

In 1986, [H.A.] Nasrallah et al. reported brain atrophy in adult males treated with amphetamines as children, concluding: "since all of the HK/MBD [hyperkinetic/minimal brain dysfunction] patients had been treated with psychostimulants, cortical atrophy may be a long-term adverse effect of this treatment."

At the 1998 National Institutes of Health (NIH) Consensus Development Conference on ADHD, [W.B.] Carey stated: "The ADHD behaviors are assumed to be largely or entirely due to abnormal brain function. The DSM-IV [*Diagnostic and Statistical Manual of Mental Disorders*, fourth edition] does not say so but textbooks and journals do. . . .

69

What is now most often described as ADHD . . . appears to be a set of normal behavioral variations."

However [J.] Swanson and [F.X.] Castellanos, having reviewed the structural magnetic resonance imaging (MRI) research, testified: "Recent investigations provide converging evidence that a refined phenotype of ADHD/HKD (hyperkinetic disorder) is characterized by reduced size in specific neuroanatomical regions of the frontal lobes and basal ganglia." I challenged Swanson, asking: "Why didn't you mention that virtually all of the ADHD subjects were on stimulant therapy—the likely cause of their brain atrophy?" Swanson confessed this was so—that there had been no such studies of ADHD-untreated cohorts.

The Consensus Conference Panel concluded: "We do not have a valid test for ADHD . . . there are no data to indicate that ADHD is a brain malfunction." (This wording appeared in the version of the final statement of the Consensus Conference Panel distributed at the press conference in the final part of the Consensus Conference, November 18, 1998. This wording, which appeared for an indeterminate time on the NIH Web site, was subsequently removed and replaced with wording claiming "validity" for ADHD.)

In 2002, Castellanos et al. published the one and only MRI study of an ADHD-untreated group. However, because the ADHD-untreated patients were two years younger than the controls, the study was invalid, leaving stimulant treatment, not the never-validated disorder, ADHD, the likely cause of the brain atrophy.

In 2002, Daniel Weinberger, of the National Institute of Mental Health, claimed "major psychiatric diseases" are associated with "subtle but objectively characterizable changes" but could reference not a single proof.

## A Pro-Drug Lie

In 2002, the Advertisement Commission of Holland determined that the claim that ADHD is an inborn brain dysfunction was misleading and enjoined the Brain Foundation of the Netherlands to cease such representations.

In 2003, Ireland prohibited GlaxoSmithKline from claiming that the antidepressant Paxil "works by bringing serotonin levels back to normal." Wayne Goodman of the FDA acknowledged that claims that selective serotonin reuptake inhibitors correct a serotonin imbalance go "too far," but had the temerity to suggest that "this is reasonable shorthand for expressing a chemically or brain-based problem."

At an FDA hearing on March 23, 2006, I testified: "Saying any psychiatric diagnosis 'is a brain-based problem and that the medications are normalizing function' is an anti-scientific pro-drug lie." Yet this has become standard practice throughout medicine, for example, at the American Psychiatric Association, American Medical Association, American Academy of Child and Adolescent Psychiatry, American Academy of Pediatrics, Child Neurology Society, American Academy of Family Physicians, FDA, and virtually all US government health-care agencies.

Journal articles, press releases, ads, drug inserts, and research informed consent documents say, or [imply], that psychological diagnoses are abnormalities/diseases. All patients and research participants with psychological problems are led to believe they have an abnormality/disease, biasing them in favor of medical interventions, and against nonmedical interventions (e.g., love, will power, or talk therapy), which presume, as is the case, that the individual is physically and medically normal and without need of a medical/pharmaceutical intervention.

The FDA is the agency most responsible for conveying the facts needed by the public to make risk versus benefit and informed consent decisions. Instead—by protecting industry, not the public—the FDA is a purveyor of the psychiatric "disease" and "chemical imbalance" lie. This must change.

*"PTSD is being grossly under reported as these kids watch their bomb riddled buddies return home in body bags."*

# The Iraq War Has Increased the Number of Veterans with Post-Traumatic Stress Disorder

*D.E. Ford, Jeff Huber, and I.L. Meagher*

*The number of soldiers returning from Iraq with post-traumatic stress disorder (PTSD) may be seriously underreported, assert D.E. Ford, Jeff Huber, and I.L. Meagher in the following viewpoint. One explanation, they maintain, is that the stigma of PTSD remains—those who watch fellow soldiers come home wounded feel that they shouldn't complain. In addition, they argue, the government tries to ration medical care by redefining disorders and shifting responsibility for PTSD to victims. Ford, a social worker, specializes in behavioral disorders. Huber, a retired naval officer, comments on military policy. Meagher manages a PTSD blog.*

As you read, consider the following questions:

1. According to Army Surgeon General Lt. Gen. Kevin C. Kiley, how many soldiers returning from Iraq have been diagnosed with stress-related mental health problems?

2. What do the authors claim is behind former president George W. Bush's public face of "Support the Troops"?

3. According to the authors, why did Dr. Pfefferbaum and Dr. North resign from the PTSD review panel?

War is hell. Unlike the Hollywood soldiers whose stoicism and stiff upper lip signal heroism; real men and women are not uniformed machines that can perform under great stress with little consequence. Trained to be part of the superior fighting machinery of the military, they are still human, mortal and unique. The gruesome terrors of war not only damage the body but can also shatter self-image, ability to trust, and belief systems, leaving the individual disillusioned and bitter. The returning combat veteran's nervous system overloads from the assault by the stealth enemy: Post Traumatic Stress Disorder (PTSD).

The Departments of Veterans Affairs' Center for PTSD defines and describes PTSD:

> ... PTSD, is a psychiatric disorder that can occur following the experience or witnessing of life-threatening events such as military combat, natural disasters, terrorist incidents, serious accidents, or violent personal assaults like rape. People who suffer from PTSD often relive the experience through nightmares and flashbacks, have difficulty sleeping, and feel detached or estranged, and these symptoms can be severe enough and last long enough to significantly impair the person's daily life.
>
> PTSD is marked by clear biological changes as well as psychological symptoms. PTSD is complicated by the fact that it frequently occurs in conjunction with related disorders

such as depression, substance abuse, problems of memory and cognition, and other problems of physical and mental health. The disorder is also associated with impairment of the person's ability to function in social or family life, including occupational instability, marital problems and divorces, family discord, and difficulties in parenting.

At least 30% of Operation Enduring Freedom and Operation Iraqi Freedom soldiers have been diagnosed with stress-related mental health problems which impair social, occupational, and interpersonal functioning according to the Army Surgeon General Lt. Gen. Kevin C. Kiley, who estimates that 5% have developed PTSD, an estimate significantly lower than other leading experts have reported. In testimony before Congress in April 2005, Kiley testified that progress was being made into how the disorder was perceived:

> We are embracing the diagnosis of PTSD . . . MHS [military health system] and VA [Department of Veterans Affairs] are embracing it rather than taking that diagnosis and excluding it and looking for some other diagnosis. That's a major cultural, medical shift.

However, in October 2005, he acknowledged, in reference to post-traumatic stress disorder in the Army, that "There's no question there is still a stigma." Still, efforts such as including post-deployment screening, stress assessment, combat stress control teams joining troops in combat, and training leadership in addressing PTSD are all good beginnings. But are there domestic forces undermining the military's attempts to combat PSTD? Are our soldiers receiving the very best treatment upon their return home? Behind the Bush Administration's public face of "Support the Troops," political agendas compete with the needs of the veterans.

The escalating price tag on the Iraq war has been projected into the trillions. Nobel prize–winning economist Joseph Stiglitz and Harvard budget expert Linda Bilmes included projected healthcare and disability costs and the impact on the economy in their estimates. And, as Stiglitz and Bilmes

noted, their estimates are conservative; the actual costs could run much higher. Thus, it's no surprise that evidence suggests that budget pressure and ideology have motivated the Bush administration to enact cost cutting measures aimed at limiting combat damaged troops' access to benefits. By its aggressive management of the public relations problems generated by the increasingly unpopular war, our government has sought to veil the death and destruction from public view. In what amounts to the Swift-boating of the American veteran, battlefield damage is minimized while operatives plant stories in the media to trumpet the view that the source of PTSD resides solely within the individual and not with the war itself. The soldiers hailed as heroic upon deployment find themselves, upon their return, portrayed as psychologically impaired *before* they went to war, morally weak, or untruthful, malingering veterans.

## Penny Wise & Pound Foolish

President Bush's economic advisor Larry Lindsay was forced to resign in December 2002 when he suggested the war could cost as much as $200 billion; thus, presumably there are intense incentives to cut costs. Powerful ideologues carefully positioned within the administration are enacting measures that would do so, not through diligent budgetary oversight of all military expenditures which have been rife with massive financial irregularities, but instead by limiting veterans' benefits. This agenda to ration care, to redefine disorders in such a way to deny the need for medical intervention, and to malign the victims unduly taxes and spends a national treasure: the well-being of our military personnel.

> The kids coming back from Iraq and Afghanistan, all of them in harm's way, deserve to come back to 21st century medical care. Whatever the cost, we need to incur that cost to provide world-class medical care to the extraordinary men and women who are in harm's way.

> August 25, 2005

> Anthony J. Principi, Former Secretary of Veterans Affairs 2001–2005

Principi's forceful support for veterans' healthcare benefits was made as he announced the closing of the aged Walter Reed Army Hospital and the opening of a new billion dollar facility in Bethesda, Maryland. Principi, whose two sons served in Iraq and under whose advocacy the Veterans Affairs budget grew from $48 billion to $65 billion in three years, resigned from the VA on 11/16/04, shortly after the reelection of President Bush.

On 1/26/05 President Bush replaced Principi with Jim Nicholson, former Chairman of the Republican National Committee from 1997–2000 and Ambassador to the Vatican, a real estate lawyer and developer with no healthcare experience. The Department of Veterans Affairs has as its stated goal ". . . to provide excellence in patient care, veterans' benefits and customer satisfaction." In classic foreshadowing of the isolation veterans feel from the decision-making processes of the do I have to complain when the guys next to me died." We are seeing a small number of the physically injured in the media, but the traumatized are nearly invisible in many ways.

## Blue Ribbon Blues

Particularly worrisome to veterans groups are the blue ribbon panels. The VA announced via a press release from Senator Larry Craig's office that it has entered into an agreement with the Institute of Medicine (IOM), an arm of the National Academy of Sciences, who have convened a blue ribbon panel to conduct a review of the assessment and diagnosis of PTSD, followed by a review of treatment and compensation practices. The IOM is a private, nonprofit organization. Veterans groups may have valid reasons for concern as blue ribbon panels have been known to be "too close to private industry." Love adds:

> After 7 years of working with the IOM's many committees, I'm firmly convinced that they just want another paying contract-so they will write in favor of the contractor rather than genuine medical issues in favor of the veteran. When these studies were started in 2005, the IOM staff even tried to hide the fact of the public meetings even from the National Veteran Service Organizations. Only after I challenged them earlier last year did they circulate that these meetings were public. 2005 was no different than any other year with the IOM, and they even let the contractor (VA, Mark Brown) dress down the only veteran in the room. To try and run me off during the opening meeting. Granted the panel tried to give me false hope in the beginning as if they were interested in any external content. But as the year progressed the panel staff became adversarial until the November 15th 2005 Government Reform hearing where they became outright belligerent. That's where they were called into question on their choice of review materials in Gulf War medical research. They are NOT the friend of the veterans, and have

VA, on 2/16/05 Nicholson convened a meeting of the Advisory Committee on Homeless Veterans in the Tropical Room at San Juan Puerto Rico's Caribe Hilton Hotel rather than in the arguably more appropriate (considering the concerns about finances), frugal confines of a room at 810 Vermont Avenue NW, Washington, D.C. And Nicholson stunned the veterans community in August 2005 when he asserted that most sufferers from Post Traumatic Stress Disorder (PTSD) can be cured, a contention unsupported by the scientific literature. In fact, the official VA site itself states that there is no cure.

In early 2005, House Republican leaders ousted a strong supporter of increased funding for veterans' benefits, Rep. Chris Smith (R-NJ) as chair and as a member of the Veterans Affairs Committee, replacing him with a choice strongly opposed by veterans groups, Rep. Steve Buyer (R-IN), whose website boasts is a ". . . leader in the fight to reduce government spending." Senator Arlen Specter (R-PA) shifted from chair of the Senate Committee on Veterans Affairs to the Judiciary Committee and Larry Craig (R-ID) was appointed chair in his place. Craig was given a 0% rating by the American Public Health Association in 2003 for having an anti-public health voting record.

It is noteworthy that there is a direct link between Craig and the Cato Institute, a libertarian think tank which advocates reducing government funding of healthcare. The Cato Institute's director of health policy is none other than Michael F. Cannon, who served under Larry Craig's direction as health policy analyst in the Senate Republican Policy Committee. Remember Cannon's name as his policy influence may be seen in proposals for PTSD treatment.

The parsimony agenda at the Veterans Health Administration has been marred by scandal, most notably by Bush appointee Dr. Nelda Wray, recruited from the Houston VA and the health-outcomes research unit at Baylor University School of Medicine. She created a stir in the research community when, newly installed in 2003 as Chief Research and Development officer, she moved VA research away from the hard science of basic research to outcomes research (which supports the cost cutting and limited utilization goals of managed care), and tried to put funding decisions in the hands of cherry picked experts instead of using the traditional peer review process. Wray was dismissed after misappropriating $1.7 million in funds provided by the pharmaceutical industry, taking inappropriate trips to Houston, using expensive lodging and transportation, creating an environment of fear in her agency, and funneling a $750,000 contract to her colleague in Houston in violation of VA regulations.

The official investigation revealed that she had extravagantly spent the pharmaceutical funds maintained by the Friends Research Institute, Inc. in an unofficial relationship and ". . . this spending constituted an illegal augmentation of the Department's appropriations, and a misuse of position." The Research and Development Office CFO, John Bradley reported that ". . . Dr. Wray did not accept being questioned, and that 'bad things' happened to those who questioned her." Criminal charges were never filed.

## The PTSD Tsunami

While Army Surgeon General Lt. Gen. Kevin Kiley acknowledges that 30% of returning troops have stress-related mental health problems, these problems are being redefined and minimized by "military medical officials" as "normal reactions to combat." These same unnamed military medical officials "cautioned against people reading their data as suggesting the war had driven so many soldiers over the edge." With Army suicide rates and heavy alcohol use increasing, barriers that prevent the majority of the afflicted from seeking treatment have been identified. In the comprehensive *New England Journal of Medicine* study "Combat Duty in Iraq and Afghanistan, Mental Health Problems, and Barriers to Care" (Hoge, et al.), these

barriers are as diverse as the perceived stigma of being seen weak and treated differently by unit leaders and membe skepticism that the use of mental health services is confide tial; and inconsistent rulings and lengthy delays in obtaini disability and other benefits. Veterans' advocate Kirt P. Lov notes:

> DOD/VA still use the old trick of patronizing a person into walking away. I've experienced it myself with VA in my own medical dealings. It is so easy with a soldier who is already irritable and excitable. The doctor says something demeaning, the soldier blows up, walks out, and the doctor writes on the computer hospital notes the soldier is violent and non-responsive. Afterwards, the soldier is haunted by that field note in his medical folder that grants VA the ability to keep him at bay or even restrain him. Forced psychiatric observation, which keeps the soldier from coming back. It's a trap that most soldiers never see coming. These kids are driven to denial from almost every direction in the bad cases.

There has been recent speculation that the VA is under pressure to report low rates of PTSD for the public relations needs of Mr. Bush's war agenda. Kirt Love[1] adds:

> As we speak, DOD is rapid chaptering 100's of medical cases out of Iraq. More than 10,000 injuries have taken place in Iraq alone, and yet it looks like that rather than medical chapters—many are just being rushed out with nothing. The stories here at Fort Hood are quite disturbing, and yet because soldiers are taught "tough guy medicine"-they don't want to complain because they look weak. Which is very much to DOD's advantage. So it looks like the Pre/Post deployment medical screenings (PL 105-85) aren't being done right to track these soldiers as they transition back to civilian life. About 23% look like they are slipping through the system. No doubt PTSD is being grossly under reported as these kids watch their bomb riddled buddies return home in body bags. You can imagine many are thinking "what right

abused the letter of PL 105-368 that assigned them the Gulf War contracts—PTSD included. This is why even the Service groups have stopped attending these meetings, just about no one in Washington DC respects the IOM these days but the contractors. DOD, VA.

The PTSD review panel has likewise come under fire for not including even one member with experience with PTSD in combat populations. Two members of the panel, who had contributed to an exhaustive review of the literature on PTSD for the American Psychiatric Association (APA) on 11/04, resigned shortly after the start of the panel's first meeting on 5/9/05. Betty Pfefferbaum, M.D. J.D, one of a nine-member work group that conducted the APA review, resigned 5/18/05. Carol North M.D., M.P.E, and a frequent research partner of Dr. Pfefferbaum, resigned her position 7/29/05 following the 7/11/05 meeting. When contacted for comment, Dr. Pfefferbaum replied, "I resigned before the IOM process actually began because my time commitments do not permit me to work on projects that are not directly applicable to my areas of interest (primarily disaster trauma, terrorism, and children) and because I did not feel I had sufficient expertise in the area to make meaningful contributions."[2] That she had sufficient expertise to contribute to the literature review for the American Psychiatric Association would seem to contradict this reasoning.

Dr. North reported that "In what seems to be unfortunate timing for my work with the IOM committee, I took a full time position at the Dallas VA in conjunction with a new job I started at UT Southwestern Medical Center in Dallas this fall. Obviously, my new VA affiliation could provide the appearance of conflict or bias with the committee's agenda, and the IOM has a policy of not having members on their committees who receive their salary from the sponsor of the study."[3] She resigned two and a half months after the start of the study. It is indeed unfortunate that it was required that

she depart due to her unique position with the very population in scrutiny. That her VA affiliation is considered a "conflict of interest" no doubt adds to the skepticism of veterans'
organizations.

The APA literature review that Dr. Pfefferbaum and Dr.
North contributed to recommends that PTSD treatment must
have one person to coordinate a team approach and that "Because of the diversity and depth of medical knowledge and
expertise required for this oversight function, a psychiatrist
may be optimal for this role, although this staffing pattern
may not be possible in some health care settings"(p.12, emphasis added by authors). The relationship between the Senate
Committee on Veterans Affairs under the chairmanship of
Larry Craig and the Cato Institute healthcare policy (a policy
which advocates deregulating the provision of healthcare and
allowing its allocation to non-MD and unlicensed providers in
order to drive down costs) under the directorship of Michael
F. Cannon may provide an additional layer of meaning to the
two psychiatrists' departures.

The competing agendas of budget, public relations and
ideology overrun veterans' needs. Those in positions of power
whose ideology embraces limited utilization of healthcare
benefits, the deregulation of healthcare providers, and the reduction in federal spending for healthcare contribute to the
deterioration of the provision of healthcare to our returning
veterans. And all those President's men can't put Johnny back
together again with a yellow ribbon.

## Notes

1. Private e-mail to D.E. Ford dated January 16, 2006
2. Private e-mail to D.E. Ford dated December 30, 2005
3. Private e-mail to D.E. Ford dated December 30, 2005

VA, on 2/16/05 Nicholson convened a meeting of the Advisory Committee on Homeless Veterans in the Tropical Room at San Juan Puerto Rico's Caribe Hilton Hotel rather than in the arguably more appropriate (considering the concerns about finances), frugal confines of a room at 810 Vermont Avenue NW, Washington, D.C. And Nicholson stunned the veterans community in August 2005 when he asserted that most sufferers from Post Traumatic Stress Disorder (PTSD) can be cured, a contention unsupported by the scientific literature. In fact, the official VA site itself states that there is no cure.

In early 2005, House Republican leaders ousted a strong supporter of increased funding for veterans' benefits, Rep. Chris Smith (R-NJ) as chair and as a member of the Veterans Affairs Committee, replacing him with a choice strongly opposed by veterans groups, Rep. Steve Buyer (R-IN), whose website boasts is a ". . . leader in the fight to reduce government spending." Senator Arlen Specter (R-PA) shifted from chair of the Senate Committee on Veterans Affairs to the Judiciary Committee and Larry Craig (R-ID) was appointed chair in his place. Craig was given a 0% rating by the American Public Health Association in 2003 for having an anti-public health voting record.

It is noteworthy that there is a direct link between Craig and the Cato Institute, a libertarian think tank which advocates reducing government funding of healthcare. The Cato Institute's director of health policy is none other than Michael F. Cannon, who served under Larry Craig's direction as health policy analyst in the Senate Republican Policy Committee. Remember Cannon's name as his policy influence may be seen in proposals for PTSD treatment.

The parsimony agenda at the Veterans Health Administration has been marred by scandal, most notably by Bush appointee Dr. Nelda Wray, recruited from the Houston VA and the health-outcomes research unit at Baylor University School of Medicine. She created a stir in the research community when, newly installed in 2003 as Chief Research and Development officer, she moved VA research away from the hard science of basic research to outcomes research (which supports the cost cutting and limited utilization goals of managed care), and tried to put funding decisions in the hands of cherry picked experts instead of using the traditional peer review process. Wray was dismissed after misappropriating $1.7 million in funds provided by the pharmaceutical industry, taking inappropriate trips to Houston, using expensive lodging and transportation, creating an environment of fear in her agency, and funneling a $750,000 contract to her colleague in Houston in violation of VA regulations.

The official investigation revealed that she had extravagantly spent the pharmaceutical funds maintained by the Friends Research Institute, Inc. in an unofficial relationship and ". . . this spending constituted an illegal augmentation of the Department's appropriations, and a misuse of position." The Research and Development Office CFO, John Bradley reported that ". . . Dr. Wray did not accept being questioned, and that 'bad things' happened to those who questioned her." Criminal charges were never filed.

## The PTSD Tsunami

While Army Surgeon General Lt. Gen. Kevin Kiley acknowledges that 30% of returning troops have stress-related mental health problems, these problems are being redefined and minimized by "military medical officials" as "normal reactions to combat." These same unnamed military medical officials "cautioned against people reading their data as suggesting the war had driven so many soldiers over the edge." With Army suicide rates and heavy alcohol use increasing, barriers that prevent the majority of the afflicted from seeking treatment have been identified. In the comprehensive *New England Journal of Medicine* study "Combat Duty in Iraq and Afghanistan, Mental Health Problems, and Barriers to Care" (Hoge, et al.), these barriers are as diverse as the perceived stigma of being seen as weak and treated differently by unit leaders and members; skepticism that the use of mental health services is confidential; and inconsistent rulings and lengthy delays in obtaining disability and other benefits. Veterans' advocate Kirt P. Love[1] notes:

> DOD/VA still use the old trick of patronizing a person into walking away. I've experienced it myself with VA in my own medical dealings. It is so easy with a soldier who is already irritable and excitable. The doctor says something demeaning, the soldier blows up, walks out, and the doctor writes on the computer hospital notes the soldier is violent and non-responsive. Afterwards, the soldier is haunted by that field note in his medical folder that grants VA the ability to keep him at bay or even restrain him. Forced psychiatric observation, which keeps the soldier from coming back. It's a trap that most soldiers never see coming. These kids are driven to denial from almost every direction in the bad cases.

There has been recent speculation that the VA is under pressure to report low rates of PTSD for the public relations needs of Mr. Bush's war agenda. Kirt Love[1] adds:

> As we speak, DOD is rapid chaptering 100's of medical cases out of Iraq. More than 10,000 injuries have taken place in Iraq alone, and yet it looks like that rather than medical chapters—many are just being rushed out with nothing. The stories here at Fort Hood are quite disturbing, and yet because soldiers are taught "tough guy medicine"-they don't want to complain because they look weak. Which is very much to DOD's advantage. So it looks like the Pre/Post deployment medical screenings (PL 105-85) aren't being done right to track these soldiers as they transition back to civilian life. About 23% look like they are slipping through the system. No doubt PTSD is being grossly under reported as these kids watch their bomb riddled buddies return home in body bags. You can imagine many are thinking "what right

do I have to complain when the guys next to me died." We are seeing a small number of the physically injured in the media, but the traumatized are nearly invisible in many ways.

## Blue Ribbon Blues

Particularly worrisome to veterans groups are the blue ribbon panels. The VA announced via a press release from Senator Larry Craig's office that it has entered into an agreement with the Institute of Medicine (IOM), an arm of the National Academy of Sciences, who have convened a blue ribbon panel to conduct a review of the assessment and diagnosis of PTSD, followed by a review of treatment and compensation practices. The IOM is a private, nonprofit organization. Veterans groups may have valid reasons for concern as blue ribbon panels have been known to be "too close to private industry." Love adds:

> After 7 years of working with the IOM's many committees, I'm firmly convinced that they just want another paying contract-so they will write in favor of the contractor rather than genuine medical issues in favor of the veteran. When these studies were started in 2005, the IOM staff even tried to hide the fact of the public meetings even from the National Veteran Service Organizations. Only after I challenged them earlier last year did they circulate that these meetings were public. 2005 was no different than any other year with the IOM, and they even let the contractor (VA, Mark Brown) dress down the only veteran in the room. To try and run me off during the opening meeting. Granted the panel tried to give me false hope in the beginning as if they were interested in any external content. But as the year progressed the panel staff became adversarial until the November 15th 2005 Government Reform hearing where they became outright belligerent. That's where they were called into question on their choice of review materials in Gulf War medical research. They are NOT the friend of the veterans, and have

abused the letter of PL 105-368 that assigned them the Gulf War contracts—PTSD included. This is why even the Service groups have stopped attending these meetings, just about no one in Washington DC respects the IOM these days but the contractors. DOD, VA.

The PTSD review panel has likewise come under fire for not including even one member with experience with PTSD in combat populations. Two members of the panel, who had contributed to an exhaustive review of the literature on PTSD for the American Psychiatric Association (APA) on 11/04, resigned shortly after the start of the panel's first meeting on 5/9/05. Betty Pfefferbaum, M.D. J.D, one of a nine-member work group that conducted the APA review, resigned 5/18/05. Carol North M.D., M.P.E, and a frequent research partner of Dr. Pfefferbaum, resigned her position 7/29/05 following the 7/11/05 meeting. When contacted for comment, Dr. Pfefferbaum replied, "I resigned before the IOM process actually began because my time commitments do not permit me to work on projects that are not directly applicable to my areas of interest (primarily disaster trauma, terrorism, and children) and because I did not feel I had sufficient expertise in the area to make meaningful contributions."[2] That she had sufficient expertise to contribute to the literature review for the American Psychiatric Association would seem to contradict this reasoning.

Dr. North reported that "In what seems to be unfortunate timing for my work with the IOM committee, I took a full time position at the Dallas VA in conjunction with a new job I started at UT Southwestern Medical Center in Dallas this fall. Obviously, my new VA affiliation could provide the appearance of conflict or bias with the committee's agenda, and the IOM has a policy of not having members on their committees who receive their salary from the sponsor of the study."[3] She resigned two and a half months after the start of the study. It is indeed unfortunate that it was required that

she depart due to her unique position with the very population in scrutiny. That her VA affiliation is considered a "conflict of interest" no doubt adds to the skepticism of veterans'
organizations.

The APA literature review that Dr. Pfefferbaum and Dr.
North contributed to recommends that PTSD treatment must
have one person to coordinate a team approach and that "Because of the diversity and depth of medical knowledge and
expertise required for this oversight function, a psychiatrist
may be optimal for this role, although this staffing pattern
may not be possible in some health care settings"(p.12, emphasis added by authors). The relationship between the Senate
Committee on Veterans Affairs under the chairmanship of
Larry Craig and the Cato Institute healthcare policy (a policy
which advocates deregulating the provision of healthcare and
allowing its allocation to non-MD and unlicensed providers in
order to drive down costs) under the directorship of Michael
F. Cannon may provide an additional layer of meaning to the
two psychiatrists' departures.

The competing agendas of budget, public relations and
ideology overrun veterans' needs. Those in positions of power
whose ideology embraces limited utilization of healthcare
benefits, the deregulation of healthcare providers, and the reduction in federal spending for healthcare contribute to the
deterioration of the provision of healthcare to our returning
veterans. And all those President's men can't put Johnny back
together again with a yellow ribbon.

## Notes

1. Private e-mail to D.E. Ford dated January 16, 2006
2. Private e-mail to D.E. Ford dated December 30, 2005
3. Private e-mail to D.E. Ford dated December 30, 2005

> *"We can expect to see a seventy-fold in-crease in PTSD over the next decade? This is an astounding (and unrealistic) amplification."*

# The Iraq War Has Not Increased the Number of Veterans with Post-Traumatic Stress Disorder

*Sally Satel*

*In the following viewpoint, Sally Satel argues that while post-traumatic stress disorder (PTSD) is a real disorder, the number of veterans returning from Iraq afflicted with the disorder is exaggerated. Estimates based on the number of postwar Vietnam veterans suffering from PTSD are flawed, she claims. Moreover, practitioners should promote rehabilitation rather than disability. In fact, she reasons that the vast majority of those returning from Iraq and Afghanistan will adjust. It is unfair to impose on these veterans the legacy of Vietnam, she asserts. Satel, a physician, is a scholar with the libertarian American Enterprise Institute.*

Sally Satel, "Post-Traumatic Stress Disorder and Iraq Veterans: Testimony before the House Committee on Veterans Affairs," *American Enterprise Institute*, March 11, 2004. Reproduced by permission of the author.

As you read, consider the following questions:

1. In Satel's opinion, how do long-range studies of people affected by the Oklahoma City bombing contradict the postwar explosion in Vietnam cases?

2. According to the author, with what does a well-advertised syndrome such as PTSD provide many unhappy, but not necessarily traumatized, people?

3. What factors does the author claim may protect against PTSD?

Post-traumatic stress disorder [PTSD] is a real and painful condition. Undoubtedly, it will afflict some men and women returning from Iraq. A humane and grateful country must treat them. But how many will be afflicted is difficult to know at this time.

It is generally put forth as an established truth—that roughly one-third of returnees from Vietnam suffered PTSD. This is at best debatable, given that fifteen percent were assigned to combat units. As we try to help the soldiers of Operation Iraqi Freedom meld back into society, it would be a mistake to rely too heavily on the conventional wisdom about Vietnam.

I will first discuss the questions raised by the government-mandated study on war stress among Vietnam veterans. Second, I will put forth some clinical and social principles for responding to the soldiers who are now rotating home.

## Studying Vietnam Veterans

The National Vietnam Veterans Readjustment Study [NV-VRS]: The Research Triangle Institute (under contract from the Veterans Affairs Administration) released the study in 1990. It concentrated on post-traumatic stress disorder, a psychiatric condition marked by disabling painful memories, anxiety and phobias after a traumatic event like combat, rape or other extreme threats.

The NVVRS found that 31 percent of soldiers who went to Vietnam, or almost one million troops, succumbed to PTSD after their return. The count climbed to fully half if one included those given the diagnosis of "partial" post-traumatic stress disorder.

On closer inspection, however, these figures are shaky. As I mentioned, only 15 percent of troops in Vietnam were assigned to combat units, so it is odd that 50 percent suffered symptoms of war trauma. True, non-combat jobs like driving trucks put men at risk for deadly ambush, but Army studies on psychiatric casualties during the war found the vast majority of cases referred to field hospitals did not have combat-related stress at all. Rather, most were sent for psychiatric attention because of substance abuse and behavioral problems unrelated to battle.

Moreover, during the years of the most intense fighting in Vietnam, 1968–69, psychiatrists reported that psychiatric casualties numbered between 12 and 15 soldiers per thousand, or a little more than 1 percent. If the 1990 readjustment study is correct, the number afflicted with diagnosable war stress multiplied vastly in the years after the war. Again, it does not add up.

How to explain the postwar explosion in Vietnam cases? The frequently proffered answer is that the start of the disorder can be delayed for months or years. This belief, however, has no support in epidemiological studies. And consider the striking absence of delayed cases in long-range studies like that of people affected by the Oklahoma City bombing [of the Alfred P. Murrah Federal Building in 1995]. Such studies have found that symptoms almost always develop within days of the traumatic event and, in about two-thirds of sufferers, fade within a year. . . .

## Reasons to Be Skeptical

There are a couple of other reasons to be skeptical. A well-advertised syndrome like PTSD could have provided a medicalized explanation for many unhappy, but not necessarily traumatized, veterans who had been trying to make sense of their experience. This seems particularly relevant to NVVRS subjects who seldom sought care or compensation. Such "effort at meaning" is a deeply human—and well-documented phenomenon.

In addition, the NVVRS researchers did not measure degree of impairment in the subjects interviewed. Nor were frequency of symptoms recorded. There is an active debate in the psychiatric literature about over-diagnosis (of many conditions, not just PTSD) prompted by the fact that clinicians or epidemiologists do not always take into account the degree of impairment associated with symptoms. After all, it is not uncommon for some people to have symptoms (e.g., nightmares, painful memories) but to function at a very high level and neither they nor those around them consider them sick. Having too low a threshold for diagnosing pathology was not uncommon at the VA where I worked. I saw, for example, a number of troubled middle-aged veterans who had only minor complaints of nightmares or occasional disturbing thoughts of Vietnam who find themselves misdiagnosed with PTSD. The most recent edition of the Diagnostic and Statistical Manual requires presence of impairment or great suffering. It is very possible that the NVVRS had too low a threshold for diagnosing PTSD.

## Relying on Self-Report

Also, the NVVRS relied heavily on self-report. Psychological studies, however, have shown how fallible memory can be. For example, people tend to reconstruct the past in terms of the present—they often exaggerate the degree of earlier misfortune if they are feeling bad, or minimize old troubles if they are feeling good. A 1997 report in the *American Journal of Psychiatry* by West Haven VA psychiatrists Steven Southwick,

Dennis Charney and C. Andrew Morgan examined Desert Storm veterans at one month and two years after their return to the U.S.

In the group, memory for traumatic events changed from first to second assessment for 88 percent of them (70 percent recalled a traumatic event at two years that they did not mention at the first month evaluation; 46 percent mentioned a traumatic event at one month but not at two years). Veterans with the most PTSD symptoms, the authors wrote, "tend to amplify their memory for traumatic events over time" though are probably unaware how those memories had changed. In other words, individuals with more severe symptoms of anxiety and depression remember a traumatic event as being worse when they are asked about it a second time than when asked about it earlier. Those with fewer symptoms, however, tended to recall the event as less harrowing than they had previously described it. This observation—from other studies of car accident victims, witnesses to a school shooting, international peacekeepers—are remarkably consistent. . . .

Relevance to today? Keep in mind that subjects were interviewed for the NVVRS at least a decade after return from Vietnam. Its questionable findings notwithstanding, the study bears little on immediately returning veterans because it measured symptoms present in veterans when they were a decade or more, not weeks, away from being overseas. . . .

But the most informative glimpse at what is happening now come from a report released [in 2004]. The VHA [Veterans Health Administration] Office of Public Health and Environmental Hazards, Report #4 (March 9, 2004), states that 436 soldiers out of 107,540 separated from active duty in Iraq have thus far been diagnosed with PTSD. This is about .4% of veterans who returned. According to adherents of the NVVRS, we can expect to see a seventy-fold increase in PTSD over the next decade? This is an astounding (and unrealistic) amplification.

## War and Trauma

War is a mother lode of traumatic experiences and the chief source of the concept of PTSD [post-traumatic stress disorder]. In the American Civil War, the resulting symptoms were sometimes described as battle fatigue. In the First World War, it was called shell shock, and in the Second World War, combat neurosis or traumatic neurosis. Soldiers in those wars who succumbed to posttraumatic stress were sometimes regarded as weak or inadequate, but that view changed as understanding of their experiences improved. Physicians and mental health professionals came to see the symptoms as, in a sense, normal responses to abnormal circumstances. By the middle of the Korean War, [Diagnostic and Statistical Manual of Mental Disorders] DSM-I included a diagnosis of "gross stress reaction," and DSM-II described a "transient situational disturbance."

*"Rethinking Posttraumatic Stress Disorder,"*
Harvard Mental Health Letter, *August 2007.*

## Lessons Learned

*Interpreting psychological states*: Will many men and women feel dislocated, sad, bitter? Of course. They may have trouble sleeping and be distractible, even hostile. Is this psychopathology? Depending on how dysfunctional the person is and degree of persistence, it could indeed be.

*Promoting protective factors*: It is important to enumerate the factors known to protect against post-traumatic stress symptoms and PTSD. These include the benefits of a smooth reintegration of the veteran into family and community, society's appreciation for his sacrifice, minimal economic hardship, engagement in purposeful work and the ability to derive reward, or at least meaning, from the war experience, as horrible as it might have been at times. The Veterans Administration may have a role in fostering some of these factors.

*Formal vs. informal care*: Many of the returning young men and women will find comfort and support in the embrace of their families, friends, communities, and houses of worship. Those who are too anxious or depressed to function or who have started drinking or using drugs heavily should get professional help. Informal discussion groups may be an option.

What is crucial is that the help we give vets does not transform acute problems and into chronic ones. The VA itself has doubtless learned some of those lessons from its treatment of Vietnam veterans.

*Practical treatment focus*: Group or individual treatment should be focused on solving practical problems and rehabilitation and putting traumatic experiences in perspective. It should not entail repeated telling of terrifying or demoralizing stories and encourage the client to assume the identity of the psychologically crippled veteran. Inpatient treatment should be reserved for those who cannot function. Specialized inpatient PTSD units have been problematic; they seemed to facilitate regression rather than readjustment.

*Beware of the disability trap*: Also, therapists should not be predicting mental disability or pushing veterans quickly toward obtaining service connected disability payments. Not surprising, disability payments provide an economic incentive to maintain dysfunction. A veteran deemed to be fully disabled by post-traumatic stress disorder can collect $2,000 to $3,000 a month, tax free. If work is often the best therapy (it structures one's life, gives a sense of purpose and productivity, provides important social opportunities and a healthy way to get one's mind to stop ruminating about problems), then ongoing disability payments can be the route to further disability and isolation.

Once a patient gets permanent disability payment, motivation to ever hold a job declines, the patient assumes—often incorrectly—that he can no longer work, and the longer he is unemployed, the more his confidence in his ability for future work erodes and his skills atrophy. He is trapped into remaining "disabled" by the fact that he was once very ill but by no means eternally dysfunctional. (If disability benefits are unequivocally indicated, lump sum payments with or without a financial guardian might make better sense than monthly installments.)

## Maintaining Healthy Skepticism

*Enlightened skepticism is in order*: Some veterans who did enter the VA medical/disability system, as observed Paul McHugh M.D., former chairman of psychiatry at Johns Hopkins University, settled easily into the status of PTSD vet. The diagnosis "conferred a status preferable to such alternatives as personality disorder, alcoholism, or adjustment disorder."

Veterans would have been better served by a skeptical stance on the part of their therapists. Loren Pankratz, a psychologist retired from a Veterans Administration Medical Center in Oregon, has written extensively about patients who distort their history and make false attributions about the cause of their symptoms. During his 25 years as a VA psychologist, Pankratz regularly dug into the military records of World War II and Vietnam veterans who told him about especially daring or improbable exploits. Pankratz was not interested in exposing or embarrassing these men, and because he was usually able to redirect them into proper treatment, he had no need to tell them he knew their stories were dramatically embellished. Gradually, Pankratz realized that many failed to improve because they were being treated for the wrong problem. Checking records helped guide Pankratz to more appropriate therapy.

*Don't suggest pathological interpretations to fragile people*: People who are feeling fragile can be very susceptible to suggestion. From ... World War I on, psychiatrists have warned about the power of morbid expectations on soldiers and advocated that clinicians raise expectations of recovery, not disability, in those with acute psychological problems. We know, for example, that debriefing after a crisis—counselor-led groups in which victims are urged to rehash the vivid and terrifying aspects of an event—can actually impede the resolution of stress symptoms. Many times acute symptoms will be a normal and temporary, and yes, very painful, part of the readjustment phenomenon. Predicting that vast numbers of Iraq vets have a future of dysfunction ahead of them is demoralizing and risks fulfilling the prophesy.

Some soldiers will return from Iraq and Afghanistan with severe psychological problems, and we must do everything in our power to help them. The vast majority, however, will be able to adjust—and imposing on them the questionable legacy of Vietnam will not do them any service. As the British psychiatrist Simon Wessely has put it: "Generals are justly criticized for fighting the last war, not the present one. Psychiatrists should be aware of the same mistake."

# Periodical Bibliography

*The following articles have been selected to supplement the diverse views presented in this chapter.*

Arthur Allen      "Vaccine Skeptics vs. Your Kids," *Mother Jones*, September 10, 2008.

Stacy Bannerman      "A Perfect Storm: PTSD," *Foreign Policy in Focus*, March 12, 2007.

James Burns      "The Medicalizing of Education," *Teachers.Net Gazette*, June 1, 2008.

Conn Hallinan      "Shafting the Vets," *Foreign Policy in Focus*, November 10, 2006.

*Harvard Mental Health Letter*      "Rethinking Posttraumatic Stress Disorder," August 2007.

Jane Salodof MacNeil      "Reject Psychiatric View of Attention Disorders," *Pediatric News*, April 2006.

Jeremy Manier and Judith Graham      "Veterans Fight the War Within: Study Finds Post-Traumatic Stress Disorder Diagnoses Are on the Rise," *Chicago Tribune*, March 13, 2007.

Christine B. Philips      "Medicine Goes to School: Teachers As Sickness Brokers for ADHD," *PLoS Medicine*, April 11, 2006.

Elizabeth J. Roberts      "A Rush to Medicate Young Minds," *Washington Post*, October 8, 2006.

Sam Wang      "Autism Myth Lives On," *USA Today*, April 15, 2008.

Warren Zinn      "Ricochet: My Shot Made Joseph Dwyer Famous. Did It Also Help Lead to His Death?" *Washington Post*, July 13, 2008.

# How Should Behavioral Disorders Be Treated?

# Chapter Preface

The terrorist attacks of September 11, 2001, represent the largest exposure of America's children to a traumatic event. As many as 8,000 children were evacuated from schools near the World Trade Center. According to Spencer Eth, medical director of behavioral health services for the St. Vincent Catholic Medical Centers and a professor of psychiatry at New York Medical College, "Many of these children saw buildings burning, saw people falling from buildings, and they were evacuated in a time of great crisis and turmoil." In addition to those on the scene, many other children were traumatized by the deaths of parents, relatives, or other familiar adults. To examine the event's impact on these children, mental health experts worked with teachers to help identity those children who might need mental health services. Of those surveyed, about 25 percent required mental health services. While few dispute that such traumatic events can lead to a need for such help, analysts do contest how best to treat these children. Indeed, this debate mirrors the debate over how to treat adults with post-traumatic stress and other behavioral disorders.

Some mental health experts believe that cognitive-behavioral therapy (CBT) is the best way to treat childhood trauma. Children who are treated with CBT are asked to tell the story of the traumatic event until they can repeat it without experiencing disabling fear. Small children may draw pictures, while older children might tell the story in writing. In group sessions, children discuss the event under the supervision of a therapist to address any mistaken ideas concerning the event, such as blaming themselves for what happened. With very young patients, some therapists employ play therapy, using various forms of play to aid in diagnosis or treatment. CBT advocates often dismiss play therapy, despite the fact that it is the most common treatment. CBT advocate

John S. March claims that "child-centered play therapy, which is a dinosaur, [is] mostly worthless." If the play therapy involves telling the story of the trauma and facing the accompanying fears, CBT advocates admit the technique might have some benefit. "But [if] it involves shooting baskets outside with kids—which most therapists end up doing—or focusing on the parent-child relationship, it's not very helpful at all," March maintains.

Other mental health experts believe that research on child trauma therapies is inadequate and thus are not as quick to dismiss play therapy. John A. Fairbank, co-director of the National Center for Child Traumatic Stress, argues that not enough is known about the impact of trauma on children or the impact of these competing therapies. "I wouldn't call [play therapy] a dinosaur at all," Fairbank asserts. There are a wide variety of play therapies and, according to Fairbank, "I don't think we should toss them out without evaluating them." Fairbank also suggests that for some child trauma victims, antidepressants might also prove useful. The main impediment, like-minded analysts assert, is a lack of research. Schools and parents are often reluctant to sacrifice time that could be spent on academic learning to deal with social concerns, including childhood trauma. Thus, many children with problems go unnoticed and untreated, creating a large gap in the research needed to measure the success of therapies. In fact, Fairbank maintains, "there isn't any systematic screening" for childhood trauma.

Whether victims of childhood trauma are being adequately treated remains controversial. The debate over how best to treat these children is, in many ways, reflective of other debates concerning the treatment of behavioral disorders. In the following chapter, the authors contest the effectiveness of a variety of behavioral disorder treatments.

*"The scientific evidence on treatment modalities for PTSD does not reach the level of certainty that would be desired for such a common and serious condition among veterans."*

# Most Post-Traumatic Stress Disorder Therapies Are Ineffective

### Institute of Medicine

*In the following review of the studies on post-traumatic stress disorder (PTSD) treatments, the Institute of Medicine (IOM) asserts that most studies have some fatal flaw. The IOM lists PTSD treatments and offers research recommendations to better evaluate their effectiveness. For example, the IOM reports, many drug studies were funded by pharmaceutical companies. Thus, to refute claims of experimental bias, the IOM reasons that studies should be conducted in settings without potential financial or intellectual bias. In addition, the IOM argues, a more generally accepted definition of PTSD recovery would better confirm treatment success.*

Institute of Medicine, "Treatment of PTSD: An Assessment of the Evidence," *Report Brief*, October 2007. Copyright © 2007 by the National Academy of Sciences. Reproduced by permission.

As you read, consider the following questions:

1. What does the IOM argue will be required to ensure high standards of research on PTSD?

2. What subpopulations of veterans with PTSD need to be studied, according to the author?

3. What are some areas of future research the author recommends?

At the request of the Department of Veterans Affairs, the Institute of Medicine's Committee on Treatment of Posttraumatic Stress Disorder (PTSD) undertook a systematic review of the PTSD literature. After nearly 2,800 abstracts were identified, the application of inclusion criteria narrowed the list down to 90 randomized clinical trials, 37 pharmacotherapy studies, and 53 psychotherapy studies.

The principal finding of the committee is that the scientific evidence on treatment modalities for PTSD does not reach the level of certainty that would be desired for such a common and serious condition among veterans. Most studies included in the committee's review were characterized by methodologic limitations, some serious enough to affect confidence in the studies' results. The committee reached a strong consensus that additional high quality research is essential for every treatment modality.

## Pharmacotherapies

The committee concludes that the evidence is inadequate to determine efficacy in the treatment of PTSD of:

- alpha-adrenergic blocker prazosin,

- anticonvulsants,

- novel antipsychotics olanzapine and risperidone,

- benzodiazepines,

- MAOIs phenelzine and brofaromine,

- SSRIs,

- other antidepressants, and

- other drugs (naltrexone, cycloserine, or inositol).

One committee member does not concur with the committee's consensus on two conclusions—on SSRIs and novel antipsychotic medications—and offers alternate conclusions (i.e., that the evidence is suggestive of efficacy) (see Appendix H in the report).

## Psychotherapies

The committee finds that the evidence is sufficient to conclude the efficacy of exposure therapies in the treatment of PTSD.

The committee concludes that the evidence is inadequate to determine the efficacy of the following psychotherapy modalities in the treatment of PTSD:

- EMDR,

- cognitive restructuring,

- coping skills training, and

- group format psychotherapy.

The committee's findings, conclusions, and recommendations about the evidence for the treatment modalities reviewed in this report are not clinical practice guidelines. The committee does not intend to imply that, for example, exposure therapy is the only treatment that should be used in treating individuals with PTSD. The committee recognizes that the transparent presentation and assessment of evidence is just one part of the larger picture of PTSD treatment that includes many other factors. The next step in the process to-

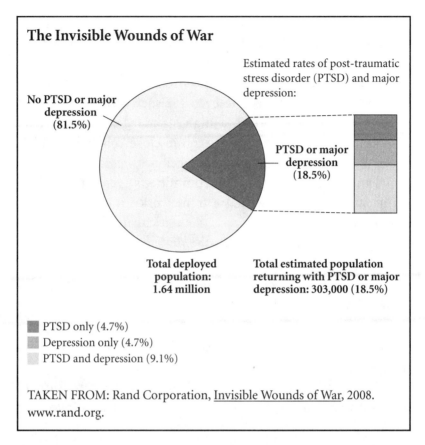

The Invisible Wounds of War

Estimated rates of post-traumatic stress disorder (PTSD) and major depression:

No PTSD or major depression (81.5%)

PTSD or major depression (18.5%)

Total deployed population: 1.64 million

Total estimated population returning with PTSD or major depression: 303,000 (18.5%)

PTSD only (4.7%)
Depression only (4.7%)
PTSD and depression (9.1%)

TAKEN FROM: Rand Corporation, Invisible Wounds of War, 2008. www.rand.org.

ward clinical decision making is making recommendations for clinical practice—a step the committee was not asked to, and did not, take.

## Recommendations for PTSD Treatment Research

The report includes eight recommendations, some developed in response to specific questions in the charge from VA, and others pertaining to treatment and research issues identified by the committee.

The committee became aware of the formidable challenges that researchers face in conducting high-quality studies of efficacy and comparative effectiveness. Nonetheless, the committee was able to identify studies that met the highest internationally accepted standards for randomized controlled trials (in assembling populations, administering treatment, measuring outcomes, and following up enrolled subjects), showing that such studies are possible even for such a difficult clinical condition as PTSD. Setting a high standard for research on PTSD and delivering on it will require close collaboration between VA and other government agencies, researchers, clinicians, and patient groups. The committee's recommendations are its suggestions for setting a framework for the future that can more successfully address the critical needs of veterans who return to civilian life with the diagnosis of PTSD.

*Treatment of PTSD has not received the level of research activity needed to support conclusions about the potential benefits of treatment modalities.*

Recommendation 1. The committee recommends that VA and other funders of PTSD research take steps to identify and require investigators to use methods that will improve the internal validity of the research, with particular attention to standardization of treatment and outcome measures, follow-up of individuals dropping out of clinical trials, and handling of missing data.

*The majority of drug studies were funded by pharmaceutical manufacturers and many of the psychotherapy studies were conducted by individuals who developed the techniques or their close collaborators. It is important to know whether these treatments would show the same effect if implemented in other settings, requiring the confirmation and replication of these research results by other investigators.*

Recommendation 2. The committee recommends that VA and other funders of PTSD treatment research seek ways to give opportunities to a broad and diverse group of investigators to ensure that studies are conducted by individuals and in settings without potential financial or intellectual conflicts of interest.

*Available research leaves significant gaps in assessing the efficacy of interventions in important subpopulations of veterans with PTSD, especially those with traumatic brain injury, major depression, other anxiety disorders, or substance abuse, as well as ethnic and cultural minorities, women, and older individuals.*

Recommendation 3. The committee recommends that VA assist clinicians and researchers in identifying the most important subpopulations of veterans with PTSD and designing specific research studies of interventions tailored to these subpopulations.

*The research on treatment of PTSD in U.S. veterans is inadequate to answer questions about interventions, settings, and lengths of treatment that are applicable in this specific population.*

Recommendation 4. The committee recommends that Congress require and ensure that resources are available for VA and other relevant federal agencies to fund quality research on the treatment of PTSD in veteran populations and that all stakeholders are included in research plans.

*Studies of PTSD interventions have not systematically and comprehensively addressed the needs of veterans with respect to efficacy of treatment and the comparative effectiveness of treatments in clinical use.*

Recommendation 5. The committee recommends that VA take an active leadership role in identifying research priorities for addressing the most important gaps in evidence in clinical efficacy and comparative effectiveness. Potential areas for future research include:

- Comparisons of psychotherapy (e.g., CBT) and medication,

- Evaluation of the comparative effectiveness of individual and group formats for psychotherapy modalities, and

- Evaluations of the efficacy of combined psychotherapy and medication, compared with either alone, and compared with control conditions. Combined treatment could be tested within study designs like those that have been applied in large studies for other psychiatric conditions.

*There is no generally accepted and used definition for recovery in PTSD; selecting appropriate outcome measures would be helpful in research on recovery.*

Recommendation 6. The committee recommends that clinicians and researchers work toward common outcome measures in three general domains that relate to recovery: loss of PTSD (Diagnostic and Statistical Manual of Mental Disorders) diagnosis, PTSD symptom improvement, and end state functioning. The committee further recommends the following three principles be considered in the selection of outcome measures:

- Validity in research,

- Convergence on a core of common outcomes for the purpose of comparability, and

- Usefulness to clinicians to assess patients over time as symptoms and function change.

The committee recommends that VA assume a leadership and convening role and work with other relevant federal agencies in developing these common approaches.

*The committee was unable to reach a conclusion on the value of intervention early in the course of PTSD based on the treatment literature it reviewed.*

Recommendation 7. The committee recommends that VA and other government agencies promote and support specific research on early intervention (i.e., reducing chronicity) in PTSD. The committee further recommends that future research specify both time since trauma exposure and duration of PTSD diagnosis, and that interventions be tested for efficacy at specific clinically meaningful intervals, as interventions might be expected to vary in effectiveness related to time since exposure and duration of diagnosis.

*The committee was unable to draw conclusions regarding optimal length of treatment with psychopharmacology or psychotherapy.*

Recommendation 8. The committee recommends that VA and other funders call for research on the optimal duration of various treatments. Trials of comparative effectiveness of different treatment lengths for those treatments found efficacious should follow. Finally, studies with adequate long-term (i.e., greater than one year) follow-up should be conducted on treatments of any length found to be efficacious.

> *"Soldiers whose commanders openly discuss the dilemmas of killing before and after combat appear to cope well with their experiences."*

# Honest Discussion About Killing Can Help Soldiers with Post-Traumatic Stress Disorder

*Adam Weinstein*

*In the following viewpoint, Adam Weinstein discusses how some analysts assert that the length of a soldier's deployment and combat experience are the best predictors of combat-related mental illness. Weinstein notes, however, that Army major Peter Kilner believes that how soldiers deal with that time and experience are the real measure. According to Kilner, those soldiers whose commanders discuss the questions raised by killing in combat are better able to cope than those who don't have that communication. Psychiatrists, as outsiders, are not as effective as combat tested officers, Kilner reasons. Weinstein attended the U.S. Naval Academy and writes for the* New York Times, Village Voice, *and* Mother Jones.

As you read, consider the following questions:

1. According to Weinstein, what giant taboo has Major Kilner broken?

2. In Weinstein's view, what personal experience led Kilner to question whether the Army had mentally prepared him to kill?

3. What does Dr. Brett T. Litz claim is "strikingly under-researched"?

In the spring of 2002, an Army major named Peter Kilner submitted an unusual essay to *Military Review*, a journal published by the Combined Arms Center in Fort Leaven-worth, Kansas. Kilner argued that combat leaders have an obligation to justify the killing their soldiers do. "Soldiers who kill reflexively in combat will likely one day reconsider their actions reflectively," he wrote. "If they are unable to justify to themselves that they killed another human being, they will likely, and understandably, suffer enormous guilt" that could balloon into post-traumatic stress disorder (PTSD). Top brass who ignored the issue, he concluded, were "treating their soldiers as commodities, not as persons."

## Breaking a Taboo

As an active-duty infantryman suggesting that a soldier's most basic task could be emotionally self-destructive, Kilner had broken a giant taboo. Not surprisingly, his article didn't go over well. Former drug czar General Barry McCaffrey, a colleague of Kilner's at West Point, dismissed his argument out of hand. "He and some of the older generation really felt like, 'Soldiers kill; they have no problem killing the enemy,'" Kilner recalls. "The question seemed to him just not a question." (McCaffrey did not respond to requests for comment.) At one point, a few of Kilner's superiors tried to discourage him from presenting his ideas publicly. "They told me it's bad PR [public relations]," he says. "I literally had a colonel pull me in the closet and threaten to break me if I spoke to the press."

But Kilner may have been on to something. Military doctors estimate that 20 percent of soldiers and 42 percent of reservists have returned from Iraq with some kind of psychological problem. Army suicides have more than doubled since 2001, hitting a 27-year high in 2007. The military has failed to address these problems in a systematic way. An investigation by National Public Radio found that the Army had punished and kicked out soldiers with PTSD; two veterans groups are currently suing the Department of Veterans Affairs for its "shameful failures" in providing mental health treatment.

In 2006, a Pentagon team concluded that the biggest predictors of mental illness were the length of a soldier's deployment and how often he experienced combat. Yet Kilner says the real issue is not the time you do, but how you deal with that time. "People don't have nightmares about, 'It's another *Groundhog Day* [a film in which the protagonist is forced to repeat living the same day over and over until he learns a moral lesson].' They have nightmares about the killing they've done and seen."

Now a lieutenant colonel, Kilner helps run the Center for Company Level Leaders at the US Military Academy at West Point. He's been interested in the ethics and impact of killing since 1994, when he was a young Airborne captain preparing to deploy to Haiti. A devout Catholic, he asked an Army chaplain what justified the killing he might do. "The president says it's right, so it's right," the chaplain replied. Kilner didn't end up killing anyone, but he wondered if the Army had mentally prepared him to do so.

## Interviewing Combat Veterans

"When the military lists wartime causes of mental illness," he told me in his office overlooking the Hudson River, "they talk about, 'Oh, it's hot; oh, it's scary,' looking at what happens to

## Warrior Codes

While there are many differences among them, warrior codes tend to share one point of agreement: the insistence that what distinguishes warriors from murderers is that warriors accept a set of rules governing when and how they kill. When they are trained for war, warriors are given a mandate by their society to take lives. But they must learn to take only certain lives in certain ways, at certain times, and for certain reasons. Otherwise, they become indistinguishable from murderers and will find themselves condemned by the very societies they were trained to serve. Individuals can fight for an objectively bad cause or a corrupt regime and still be warriors, as long as they have a warrior's code that requires them to observe the rules of war. There can be no honor in any conflict for those who believe that they have no moral obligation to restrain their behavior in any way.

*Shannon E. French,*
*"When Teaching the Ethics of War Is Not Academic,"*
The Chronicle Review, *March 21, 2003.*

soldiers without any mention of the violent things soldiers actually *do*." By interviewing combat veterans, Kilner hopes to spur an internal debate between traditionalists who say any discussion of killing undermines morale, and those who say the military is ignoring a major cause—perhaps *the* major cause—of PTSD.

One of the soldiers Kilner has talked with is Major Rob Hefner, a 42-year-old Texan who ditched a stateside post for a combat tour in Iraq. One day in June 2005, Hefner came under fire at an Iraqi army checkpoint. He spotted a figure with a rifle approximately 300 feet away. "He was gonna shoot at my soldiers," Hefner recalls. "That is not a permissible action." He raised his M-4, zeroed in on the man's chest, and fired once. "At the time I fired the shot, all I felt was the satisfaction of seeing a round hit its intended target, like being out on the range," he says.

After the firefight, Hefner went to look for the body. "I really can't answer why," he says. "Probably a part of me wanted to humanize the guy." Hefner asked the Iraqis what they intended to do with the corpse. "We don't bury dogs," one replied. "They left him there to rot, and for weeks, if the wind was right, you could smell him," Hefner says.

"I didn't regret in any way, shape, or form what I did. But neither did I delude myself by saying it was the right thing to do." He stops to think about his next words. "I'm okay with having done a wrong thing for the right reasons."

Getting soldiers like Hefner to talk is not easy, partly due to etiquette. "As crazy as it is, it's a question that's just impolite to ask," Kilner explains. When he first approached soldiers online, he recalls, "My question—'How do you justify killing to yourself?'—rubbed some people really wrong. I remember one letter started, 'Who the hell are you to question whether what I did was right or wrong?'" One soldier told Kilner that he should be spending his time "worrying about how to kill people."

## Noting a Pattern

In his research, which has included two monthlong trips to Iraq, Kilner has noted a pattern. Soldiers whose commanders openly discuss the dilemmas of killing before and after combat appear to cope well with their experiences. Soldiers who lack that support fall into isolation or depression. He paraphrases psychologist and retired Lt. Colonel David Grossman, the author of *On Killing*: "If you go into it cracked, you come out of it shattered. If you go into it strong, you come out stronger." Hefner agrees with that assessment. "Let's be honest.

Most of our trigger pullers are kids, 18, 19 years old. How many of our 18- and 19-year-olds are anything *but* cracked?"

Clinicians have paid little attention to Kilner's research, in part because it's entirely anecdotal. It is difficult to estimate how many veterans might be adversely affected by the stress of killing because the military doesn't collect statistics on how many have killed in the line of duty, not even among those who are treated for depression or PTSD.

The lasting psychological consequences of killing are "strikingly under-researched," according to Dr. Brett T. Litz, associate director of the National Center for PTSD. "Unfortunately," he says, "we are just now getting serious about scientifically evaluating the unique psychological and social scars of killing and other potentially morally injurious experiences in Iraq."

Many of the soldiers I've spoken with say that the military's response to combat stress is ineffective. The Army provides soldiers with pocket guides on combat stress that feature kernels of wisdom such as "Try to look calm and in control" and "Drink plenty of fluids." When they return from overseas, servicemen and -women are offered a questionnaire that is supposed to screen for PTSD. However, it does not ask directly if a soldier has killed anyone.

Soldiers who advocate a more honest discussion believe it can only come from their combat-tested officers and colleagues. "The answer is not more PTSD awareness and shrinks," Hefner says. "Soldiers don't need to lay on someone's couch and talk about their childhood. They need the company of other soldiers . . . After all, why does the VFW [Veterans of Foreign Wars, an organization that offers support and encourages community involvement] exist?"

Kilner agrees, but he doesn't expect the conversation to start soon. With 195,000 soldiers currently on combat tours in Iraq and Afghanistan, he explains, "Everyone's really busy."

| *"ADHD drugs may be safer in terms of the abuse potential and general medical health than the general public believes."*

# Drugs Are an Effective Treatment for Attention-Deficit/ Hyperactivity Disorder

*Norman Sussman*

*Stimulant drugs have many benefits in the treatment of attention-deficit/hyperactivity disorder (ADHD), maintains Norman Sussman in the following viewpoint. For example, he contends that they help ADHD patients focus so that they can absorb information and improve school performance. Research indicates, says Sussman, that stimulants help fine tune activity in the region of the brain that involves attention and impulse control. Moreover, he claims that stimulant drugs may in fact be safer than the public thinks. Sussman, the editor of* Primary Psychiatry, *is a psychiatry professor at New York University School of Medicine.*

Norman Sussman, "Explaining the Cognitive Enhancing Effects of Drugs that Treat ADHD" *Primary Psychiatry*, vol. 15, 2008, pp. 19–20. Copyright © 2008, Primary Psychiatry, a publication of MBL Communications. Reproduced by permission.

As you read, consider the following questions:

1. What does Sussman report are some of the reasons stimulant drugs have come into question?

2. What does the author believe will be the benefit of understanding how a drug works?

3. What did a May 2008 study published in the *American Journal of Psychiatry* suggest?

The clinical use of psychostimulants to treat attention-deficit/hyperactivity disorder (ADHD) is widespread, but the neural mechanisms responsible for their cognition-enhancing/behavioral-calming have never been adequately explained. This lack of clarity makes it more difficult to address criticisms that these drugs are not effective or are harmful. The fact is that stimulants are high on the list of controversial psychotropic medications. Apart from unanswered questions about how these drugs work, a major reason for concern about the use of drugs like amphetamines and methylphenidate is that they have a potential for diversion for recreational use, or some argue, may result in abuse among those who use them therapeutically. Another source of controversy is the fact that these agents are primarily used to treat children and adolescents with ADHD, a diagnosis that itself is actively questioned in the press. Most recently, there have been reports that influential researchers at Harvard Medical School may not have adequately disclosed the extent of their relationships with manufacturers of ADHD medications; these reports have raised additional questions about the validity of some studies that show very favorable risk-benefit profiles when these drugs are used to treat ADHD. Not being a specialist in child adolescent psychiatry, nor having ever done research or consulted for a marketer of psychostimulants, I can only make observations based on my reading of the literature, reports from my patients, and accounts from patients' family members.

## The Psychostimulants

Psychostimulants are the primary drugs used to treat ADHD [attention-deficit/hyperactivity disorder]. Although these drugs stimulate the central nervous system, they have a calming effect on people with ADHD.

These drugs include:

- Methylphenidate (Ritalin, Concerta, Metadate, Daytrana)

- Dexmethylphenidate (Focalin)

- Amphetamine-Dextroamphetamine (Adderall)

- Dextroamphetamine (Dexedrine, Dextrostat)

*University of Maryland Medical Center,*
*"Attention Deficit Hyperactivity Disorder," 2008.*

## The Benefits of Stimulants

The following are the basic benefits of stimulants. First, among hyperactive patients, the stimulants improve their ability to absorb and integrate information. They also become more focused and attentive. Second, when effective, drugs work rapidly, even within one day. A typical response is "I never thought this could be so easy." The benefits are usually unmistakable. Last, there is an improvement in self esteem as a response to improved academic performance and a reduction in household tension that may have previously arisen from failure to do homework, reports of behavioral problems in school, and sloppiness at home.

Understanding how a drug works—demystifying its mechanism of action—can go a long way in overcoming excessive skepticism or antipathy to a psychotropic agent. It can also help in the development of more effective or better-tolerated medications. It may be helpful that researchers have made recent progress in explaining how these drugs work. Findings from research on rats that appeared in *Biological Psychiatry*, for example, suggest work by "fine-tuning" neuron activity in the prefrontal cortex, the part of the brain responsible for filtering out distractions and helping people to focus on tasks. University of Wisconsin, Madison researchers Devilbiss and Berridge report that methyphenidate "fine-tunes" neuronal activity in the prefrontal cortex. This is the brain region involved in attention, decision-making, and impulse control. Of particular interest is that the medication had little or no effects on other areas of the brain.

To investigate, Devilbiss and Berridge attached tiny electrodes to individual neurons in the brains of normal rats and watched how different doses of the drug affected neuron activity. This is an important study because it seeks a more scientific explanation for the cognition-enhancing/behavioral-calming actions of these drugs.

## A More Specific Explanation

The usual response to the question of "How do these drugs work?" has been to say that they raise brain activity of the catecholamine neurotransmitters, dopamine and norepinephrine. This study provides a more complex but more specific explanation. According to the authors, the study showed that cognition-enhancing doses of methylphenidate . . .

> . . . increase the magnitude of both excitatory and inhibitory responses of pre-frontal cortex [PFC] neurons while simultaneously reducing the duration of the inhibitory response. Low-dose methylphenidate also produced 'gating,' resulting in a larger number of PFC neurons responsive to CA1-subiculum input. Combined, these observations suggest that low-dose methylphenidate increases both the sensitivity of PFC neurons and the pool of responsive PFC neurons in a

more complex manner than simply regulating the level of PFC excitability (ie, gain of neuronal activity), consistent with known actions of catecholamines on cortical neurons.

A major concern about the use of stimulants is their potential for abuse. In May 2008, the *American Journal of Psychiatry* published an article that suggested there was little or no evidence that the use of stimulants to treat children increased subsequent risk of substance abuse. The study involved [more than] 100 young men 10 years after they had been diagnosed with ADHD. The investigators reported that their findings support the hypothesis that stimulant treatment does not increase the risk for subsequent substance use disorders.

In fact, ADHD drugs may be safer in terms of abuse potential and general medical health than the general public believes. Because of unwarranted reluctance to seek help for themselves or their children, many patients suffer needless frustration, poor self-esteem, and both academic and career difficulties. I hope that, as we learn more about the underlying neurobiology of ADHD and the mechanism-of-action of drugs that treat its manifestations, the idea of seeking treatment will become more prevalent and the types of treatment options will expand.

> *"Most experienced school counselors concede that ... medication loses most of its effectiveness by the teenage years anyway, so medications are not a long-term solution for ADD."*

# Drugs Are Not a Long-Term Solution for Attention-Deficit/ Hyperactivity Disorder

*Frank Lawlis*

*Drugs are not a healthy long-term option for children diagnosed with attention deficit disorder (ADD), argues Frank Lawlis in the following viewpoint excerpted from his book* The ADD Answer: How to Help Your Child Now. *He maintains that many who prescribe ADD medication are not pediatric psychiatrists, but family doctors who are not really qualified to observe whether the drugs are working effectively, In fact, Lawlis asserts, these drugs can pose a risk to a child's cardiovascular system. In his view, a strong family environment and establishing healthy be-*

*havior is a safer and healthier long-term option. Lawlis is a psychologist, a fellow of the American Psychological Association, and a contributing psychologist for the* Dr. Phil *show.*

As you read, consider the following questions:

1. Under what conditions does the author believe ADD medications should be used?

2. What old saying does the author claim explains why most doctors recommend drugs to treat ADD?

3. In the author's opinion, what do some physicians do when psychotic symptoms appear as a result of ADD drugs?

Medical students are often warned that "sometimes the treatment can be worse than the disease." I sincerely believe that is often the case when children with ADD are given medication to control their symptoms.

ADD medications are most often prescribed by family physicians—not by a pediatric psychiatrist—which makes me very suspicious. How much understanding do such physicians have of these very potent drugs? My personal and professional opinion is that they should be used very cautiously and only on a short-term basis with specific goals in mind. Most experienced school counselors concede that such medication loses most of its effectiveness by the teenage years anyway, so medications are not a long-term solution for ADD.

## Better Options Are Available

There are better and healthier options for treating your child's ADD, beginning with a strong family environment and a focus on healthy behaviors and goals . . . and including a range of approaches to stimulate the brain and focus the child's attention naturally. . . . I base my understanding of medication on years of experience in working with children and on years of working and researching ADD. Although I have had training in psychopharmacology, I always seek recommendations from referring physicians in matters related to medication. I also want to be very clear that I do not have any direct responsibilities for issuing prescriptions or for making the necessary laboratory assessments critical to any drug protocol, especially with children. However, I consult with a group of medical experts when devising medication strategies.

Let us be fair with doctors. There is an old saying credited to Abraham Maslow, a famous psychologist: "If the only tool that you have is a hammer, everything looks like a nail." Physicians nowadays are asked to evaluate and treat hundreds of childhood problems, and most feel that the only tools they have are drugs. Doctors also rarely observe the daily behavior of the child who is being treated. They usually have to rely on the observations and opinions of parents and teachers—not only as a basis for diagnosis but also for evaluating the results. Too often the only feedback the doctor receives on medication is that the parent no longer brings the child in to see him. If the physician doesn't hear anything more, he assumes the medication worked properly. But in truth, it could be that the parents simply looked elsewhere for help, or gave up.

## The Circular Firing Squad

Too often when a child has ADD, everyone responsible for helping him is shooting in the dark. Doctors often don't get good follow-up information. Parents get frustrated and make decisions without adequate professional input. Instead of circling the wagons against ADD, we form a circular firing squad and shoot at one another.

Typically, parents, physicians, and teachers find themselves at odds over a child's treatment. Parents are often bewildered about what to do to help and protect their child. School administrators, understandably, are most concerned about the

## A Mother's Fears

A single mother of three young boys . . . once vowed that she would go to jail before she would abide them being prescribed the attention deficit hyperactivity disorder drug Ritalin. She believed that shoot-from-the-hip diagnoses of attention deficit disorder, attention deficit hyperactivity disorder and trendy mental disorders du jour unfairly stigmatize boys whose high energy and impulsiveness was in times past dismissed simply as "boys being boys."

*Gerald K. McOscar, "ADHD,"*
*Ifeminists.com, May 24, 2006.*

learning environment for all of their students. Too often, busy physicians treat the symptoms, not the child.

That is madness. But it is understandable madness and it is prevalent. We are a pill-popping, quick-fix society. School administrators are under pressure themselves to get classrooms under control. Few physicians are trained adequately to deal with ADD children. I have attended medical conferences on ADD in which the doctors on the dais obviously had no clue about the long-term adverse effects of medicating children. It is a very serious business, especially when dealing with any drugs that affect a child's neurological system.

Until recently, no studies systemically examined the long-term effects of drugs on children, such as Ritalin and amphetamines (Dexedrine and Adderall). Some of the side effects of these drugs can be profound. They can be a greater threat to a child's health than most, if not all, ADD symptoms. Certainly they can cause psychosis, including manic and schizophrenic episodes . . .

Unfortunately some physicians typically do not stop medicating when psychotic symptoms appear. Instead, they may slap on another diagnosis, of depression or antisocial personality, and then treat this diagnosis by adding antidepressants, mood stabilizers, or neuroleptics (commonly used for epilepsy) to the treatment mix. It is not unusual for children to be taking as many as five different medications, all based on adult prescriptions. Meds upon meds is madness upon madness . . .

The side effects are not restricted to psychiatric problems. Stimulants excite the whole body, not only the brain. Stimulating medications also affect the cardiovascular system. One of the side effects of Ritalin is that it boosts the activity of the heart and the cardiovascular systems so that they develop beyond what is considered normal. There is also some danger of liver damage from medications used to treat ADD and side effects. Sleep and appetite problems resulting from medication are also of concern . . .

Parents need to understand the potential dangers used to treat ADD.

> *"In mild ADHD ... a more organized and coherent system of discipline can make the difference in whether your kid will be on Ritalin or not."*

# Effective Discipline Will Help Some Children Avoid Behavioral Disorders

*Nancy Shute*

*In the following viewpoint, Nancy Shute, a staff writer for U.S. News & World Report, interviews Lawrence Diller, a behavioral pediatrician. According to Diller, stronger discipline with young children may prevent parents from having to resort to behavioral disorder drugs. He argues, however, that because modern parents often believe that all conflict with their children is bad, they often wait too long to deal with behavior problems. Diller does not advocate spanking, especially by parents who have depression or other problems. Rather, he says that a swat on the bottom of the defiant child is better than having to later resort to drugs.*

As you read, consider the following questions:

1. What motivated Diller to make his claim that a spanking is better for unruly kids than a pill?

2. What component did Diller add to Thomas Phelan's discipline program?

3. What does Diller say is a misreading of his position?

Over the years I've talked with Lawrence Diller, a behavioral pediatrician in Walnut Creek, Calif., about how society deals with children with attention deficit hyperactivity disorder [ADHD]. He often prescribes Ritalin for children with ADHD, but he also thinks that Ritalin is prescribed too often. He seems like a thoughtful, reasonable guy. So imagine my surprise when I saw an article by Diller in which he asked: "Could it be that America would rather give unruly kids a pill than a swat?" Spanking instead of Ritalin? Wow. So I called him and asked what's up. Excerpts:

## A Controversial Issue

*Nancy Shute: Spanking is probably the most controversial issue in child rearing. You treat children with ADHD. What on earth compelled you to write that spanking may not be so bad?*

Lawrence Diller: I was provoked. About a year ago, a California assemblywoman from the South Bay put out a proposal to make the spanking of children 3 years old and under criminal. I thought, please, please! The reason it gets to me is that in 30 years of practice as a developmental pediatrician, issues of discipline cause 80 percent of the problems that I see. The families that are struggling with children's behavior are also struggling with spanking. Often, they've taken a vow of abstinence. They figure if spanking is bad, then all forms of conflict are bad, and they hesitate to discipline their children. They wait too long before taking effective action. This doesn't have to be spanking; it could be removal of a toy or imposi-

tion of a timeout. I am talking about middle-class, upper-middle-class families that love their kids, that have the resources for their kids.

What gets children into trouble early on are qualities of temperament—qualities of persistence and intensity. These kids have determination, stubbornness—a simple no doesn't work. Even a "Boo!" doesn't faze these guys. The other quality of temperament that comes into play is intensity. When the child is happy they're very happy, but when they're angry they're very angry.

## Effective Discipline

*What form of discipline do you recommend to parents?*

I keep copies of the book *1-2-3 Magic* [a top-selling book by clinical psychologist Thomas Phelan] in my office. I like it a lot. [The book provides a simple system for disciplining that involves counting to three and then putting the child in timeout.] I give parents of 4-, 5- and 6-year-olds a guarantee that in 72 hours their child will be better if they follow these methods.

The component I added to Phelan's program that makes it 80 to 90 percent successful in the 6-and-under group is spanking or other physical intervention. There's good solid evidence that when you give parents permission to give one or two smacks on the child's bottom if the child defies the rules of the timeout procedure, the family is more often successful with the approach. For parents still uneasy about a spank, they can use a specific restraint technique I call "the hold" [holding a child against the parent's chest]. But kids actually prefer a spank because it's over with right away.

*But spanking's not recommended in* 1-2-3 Magic.

No. Phelan says if they don't go to timeout, start the timer again, and add another consequence. I think that's extremely hard for small children to use to make the right decision.

I prepare the parents for the likely initial very intense negative reaction from the child, and I feel that if I send them out with the 72-hour guarantee, they're strong enough to handle it. This is very important to tell the parents because otherwise many would give up. With their understanding that they are not hurting their child long term and this is what's called for to demonstrate their consistent strength and steadiness, they are ready to persevere. When children are out of control, you may be sparing this kid and family months of treatment and the risk of being labeled mentally ill. If you don't deal with the bad behavior, it takes you to ADHD-land; it takes you oppositional-defiant-disorder-land, to generalized anxiety-land, and obsessive-compulsive-disorder-land.

*One of the big concerns is that spanking will increase the physical abuse of children. Are there parents who shouldn't spank?*

Parents shouldn't spank if they have major depression, major marital problems, or substance abuse problems. They shouldn't spank in desperation or in anger—that's what leads to the negative outcomes, like increased violence, associated with corporal punishment.

## Discipline and Mild ADHD

*Aren't you worried that parents will say: Larry Diller says if I spank my kid, he won't get ADHD?*

That is my big worry. And that's why my friends tell me to keep my mouth shut.

To say that all ADHD kids should be spanked is a misreading of my position. But I expect parents and schools to do something before we give out pills. And I give out pills.

What we overlook is that in mild ADHD, which is the majority of the ADHD that is diagnosed in the community, a more organized and coherent system of discipline can make the difference in whether your kid will be on Ritalin or not. You don't have to spank. But if you're using spanking as one of an array of tools to get control of your kid, you're not hurting them in the long term. Lively, impulsive, spontaneous kids who know when to shut up don't get medicine.

Nobody wants to be pro-spanking. I just got asked to be on a website called Opposing Views, where they asked me to take the pro-spanking position. I declined. I'm not pro-spanking. I just think a well-thought-out spank ain't so bad and shouldn't be banned.

> "Most people dealing with OCD require
> a two-pronged approach of medication
> ... and a Kafkaesque form of therapy
> called exposure and response preven-
> tion."

# Obsessive-Compulsive Disorder Can Be Controlled

*Jeremy Katz*

*In the following viewpoint, Jeremy Katz maintains that one of the most successful treatments for obsessive-compulsive disorder (OCD) is exposure and response prevention therapy, in which people with OCD are exposed to the source of their anxiety in order to become desensitized to it. For example, Katz discusses how an OCD victim who feared stabbing someone was placed in ever-closer proximity to knives until they were able to stand behind someone for 90 minutes holding a knife. Katz, who has a mild case of OCD, is a staff writer for* Men's Health.

As you read, consider the following questions:

1. According to Katz, what example does Michael Jenike, M.D., provide of the agonizing nature of OCD?

Jeremy Katz, "Are You Crazy Enough to Succeed?" *Mens Health*, vol. 23, July-August 2008, p. 150. Copyright © 2008 Rodale, Inc. Reproduced by permission.

2. In the author's view, under what circumstances are behaviors not real obsessions or compulsions?

3. What are some of the drugs used along with exposure
   and response prevention to treat OCD?

I sit in the glass-walled nurses' station, waiting for my day to
begin. A steady stream of people—all living with obsessive-
compulsive disorder, or OCD—approach the half door and
utter some variation of "I have to go to the bathroom." The
attractive young woman on duty smiles and hands over a
small quantity of toilet paper, a squirt of soap in a specimen
cup, and a paper towel with a cheery "Here you are!" This is
what grade school must have seemed like to George Orwell.

Pretty soon I have to go, too. How could I not?

I'm here to interview the doctor, not seek treatment from
him, so I'm directed empty-handed to a staff bathroom in
which I discover four separate soap dispensers, a forest of paper products, and two signs about washing my hands—one to
remind me to do it, and the other to tell me how.

I'm at the Obsessive Compulsive Disorders Institute
(OCDI), a residential treatment center in McLean Hospital—
Harvard's psychiatric center—to see if my own OCD problem
wasn't just my secret but maybe also the secret to my success.
All my adult life, intrusive thoughts have alternately halted my
progress and saved my ass, and I'd finally like to separate the
bad from the good.

## An Agonizing Disorder

The medical director at the center, Michael Jenike, M.D., is
both a maverick and a pioneer in the OCD community. He
founded this facility, the first of its kind, to help sufferers of
what he considers the most agonizing of psychiatric disorders.

"I had a 17-year-old who had kidney cancer that was going to kill him in 5 or 6 months. He also had a bad case of
OCD. He said he'd rather get rid of his OCD and live only 6

months, than get rid of the cancer and live with the OCD. That's when it first hit me: This is some serious stuff."

The people seeking treatment at OCDI do not have the minstrel-show version of the disorder acted out by Tony Shalhoub in *Monk* or Jack Nicholson in *As Good as It Gets*. The institute's residents are seriously impaired. They have the kind of shattering anxiety that would make the rest of the OCD world—roughly 1 percent of all adults, 2.3 million of them in the United States alone—want to scrub their hands. The real numbers could be even higher, because OCD may be underdiagnosed and undertreated. Half of all OCD cases are serious—and that's the highest percentage among all anxiety disorders. On average, people flail about for 17 years and see three or four doctors before they find the right care.

## Adding to the Confusion

That horror aside, OCD has become cool. Perhaps it fascinates us because it forces otherwise normal people to carry out insane acts—acts that they know are insane. It has great dramatic tension. We secretly enjoy the dissonance of a perfectly rational man becoming convinced that he is fatally contaminated and washing his hands with bleach and a scrub brush, only to repeat the whole routine 10 minutes later. Paging Lady Macbeth.

And anyway, who wouldn't want a condition David Beckham has, even if it is his signature brand of mental illness? The popularization of the disorder has led to a heap of confusion. Everyone I know is "obsessed" or "compulsive" about something. And then there's the throwaway excuse of our times: "Oh, that's just my OCD."

This casual imprecision only adds to the confusion of talking about OCD. Sanjaya Saxena, M.D., an associate professor of psychiatry and behavioral sciences at the University of California at San Diego and the director of the school's OCD program, points out that "the meanings of 'compulsion' and 'obsession' as we speak of them in common parlance are not the same as the strict mental-health definitions." Obsessing about your work or your girlfriend doesn't mean you have OCD, and most people understand that "compulsively" keeping a neat desk or managing a stock portfolio is no big deal.

## Distinguishing OCD from Addiction

More to the point, those everyday fixations do not put you in danger of developing full-blown OCD. Even habits that are worrisome and possibly progressive, such as sex addiction, compulsive gambling, or overdrinking, fall within the spectrum of addictive behavior and not OCD.

Like our common, everyday infatuations, says Dr. Saxena, these habits persist "because they are rewarding in and of their own right." A true obsession, though, is "a recurrent, intrusive fear, impulse, or image that is distressing and anxiety-provoking," he says, while a compulsion is "a repetitive behavior done in response to an obsessional fear or worry and designed to prevent something bad from happening or to reduce distress."

If the behavior produces pleasure or a reward—even a strange or unhealthy reward—it's not a real obsession or compulsion, and it won't develop into one. Gerald Nestadt, M.D., a professor of psychiatry at Johns Hopkins, puts it this way: "The alcoholic may say, 'I shouldn't drink, but I love to,' whereas the person with a contamination obsession would say, 'I don't want to wash my hands, and I wish I could stop.' The reason the addictive person wants to stop is only because of the consequences, not the unwanted urge."

## The Power of Negative Thoughts

Jonathan does have OCD. He's a bright man, tall, self-possessed, funny, and utterly disabled by a disorder that has steadily taken over his life. He's living at OCDI and doing the hardest work of his life just to quiet the intrusive thoughts and maddening rituals that have been his unwelcome companions since he was 13 years old. If a negative thought—"is my father going to die?"—intruded while he performed a task, he'd have to repeat the task over and over again until he completed it without the whisper of a bad thought.

If he thought about something bad while closing the car door, says Jonathan, "I'd have to close the car door again. If I had an intrusive thought while I was going over a review on an employee, I had to rewrite it."

We all have intrusive thoughts. They flash unbidden across our mental JumboTrons, startling us with their violence, depravity, or just outright weirdness. I'd bet every New Yorker has imagined hip-checking some stranger into the path of an oncoming subway car, and that every Californian has considered, for one brief moment, the idea of plowing his SUV into the jerk in front of him on the Santa Monica Freeway.

For a person living with OCD, thoughts like these are not wadded up and tossed in the recycling bin. Instead, they are pored over, analyzed, and scrutinized for truth.

Imagine this: You've just parked the car. You hop out, grab your bag, and head toward the gym. But wait. Did you lock the car? You head back to make sure you did. Yup, it's locked. Problem solved.

Jeff Szymanski, Ph.D., OCDI's director of psychological services, explains. "Someone with OCD says, 'I went and checked the car, but did I really check it? I'm looking at my hand turning the key in the lock, but is that perception really clear enough? Did I hear the click, or do I just remember hearing the click, or did I hear the click last time I checked this?'"

Shrinks call this pathological doubting, but the person with OCD doesn't need a memo from the Department of Justice to know it's torture.

## Managing OCD

The psychosocial treatment protocol for obsessive-compulsive disorder (OCD) has been well established and empirically supported. Exposure and ritual prevention (ERP) has been found to produce successful management of symptoms in roughly 85% of OCD cases. This strategy ... has since been studied and refined by many outstanding researchers and clinicians. However, over time most behavioral therapists have added their own "personalized spin" to ERP and in some cases added other types of therapy to the mix.

*Bradley C. Riemann,*
*"How I Treat OCD," www.rogershospital.org.*

## A Personal Story

Looking back, I realize that my OCD began to appear during my senior year of high school, if not earlier. I became convinced that every girl I dated was betraying me ... nightly. And so I quizzed them on their whereabouts and demanded alibis for any unexplained absences. Oddly enough, my girlfriends found this suffocating.

My condition confined itself to that strange little corner of my world throughout my college years, and I did just fine. There are some tolerant females out there, let me tell you. But after I graduated, found a job, and moved to New York, I promptly dissolved into a puddle of anxiety.

"The core of OCD and the core of all anxiety is uncertainty. In uncertainty there is the potential for danger," Szymanski says. "OCD really has its field day in stress and in transition. Every time people with OCD go through a change, they're stuck with uncertainty. They want to make themselves certain, and they spend all their time replaying what-if scenarios." Hell, yeah. I spent 3 years of my life wondering if I had AIDS, hepatitis, and every other infection (despite my no-risk behavior and double-digit blood tests). I called the AIDS hotline so often that a counselor finally yelled at me to get off the phone. "You're worried," he said, "but the guy on the other line is dying." I lost whole days of my young adulthood thinking about what I touched, if I had a cut on my hand when I touched it, or if I'd touched my mouth or eyes before washing. Then I'd replay the whole series of events: Did I wash well enough? Am I sure I didn't have a cut?

I lived in an [graphic artist M.C.] Escher print.

When I tell Dr. Jenike these details, I don't get the "you freak!" reaction I still brace myself for. "Whatever's the most repugnant to you, that's often what the obsessive thoughts get stuck on," he says. "Like a mother nursing a baby—the mother will think I want to have sex with my baby and be horrified. It seems like OCD is looking for the most repulsive thing to torture people with."

For me, it stopped right there. I never developed the typical hand-washing, repeated-shaving, stove-checking, counting, or touching compulsions. I did not graduate to the level of thinking, "If I do this, then the thing I'm anxious about won't happen." But my girlfriend suspicions and infection worries were plenty bad enough.

Szymanski suggests thinking about it this way: "OCD rituals sound crazy. But find a place within yourself where you experience a negative emotion so powerful that you're willing to do anything—sell your mother—to get away from that emotion. Even if that behavior makes you look crazy to other people. That's the feeling of OCD."

That feeling finally drove me to a psychopharmacologist, who hit a homer on the first pitch. Prozac wiped out my symptoms within a couple of weeks. I could feel my brain returning to normal.

# A Two-Pronged Approach

But most people dealing with OCD require a two-pronged approach of medication (in the form of selective serotonin reuptake inhibitors—SSRIs—like Prozac, Luvox, or Zoloft) and a Kafkaesque [absurd and seemingly pointless] form of therapy called exposure and response prevention, or ERP. In ERP, a person learns to tolerate repeated exposure to the very cue that triggers the anxiety without acting out the attending ritual. It's administered in stages, with each stage ratcheting up the exposure.

At OCDI, residents work at dealing with their condition for hours and hours each day, all the while agreeing not to carry out the compulsive behaviors that they once used to temporarily neutralize the power of their thoughts. Each ERP is designed to address a particular obsession or compulsion. Compulsive washers will touch toilets and not be allowed to wash.

Jonathan had to listen to a loop tape, hearing, "I hope my mother will die today" while he pursued activities he enjoyed, "because the thoughts are just thoughts, there's no credence to that happening." He seems agitated and a little rote when he says this, as if the "cure" hasn't quite taken hold.

Repeated exposure to the source of the anxiety, the theory goes, will desensitize a person to it, robbing it of emotional power. In one memorable example, a person with an obsessional fear of stabbing someone was placed in ever greater proximity to knives. Eventually he graduated to standing behind an OCDI staff member for 90 minutes, holding a knife at the ready for a fatal thrust.

No one knows for certain what goes on inside the brain of a person living with OCD, but science is coming much closer to an answer. According to S. Evelyn Stewart, M.D., an assistant professor of psychiatry at Harvard medical school, brain imaging has revealed a biological underpinning for OCD: An over-active loop runs from the brain's decision center (or orbitofrontal cortex) to its movement-governing center (thalamus) and into the basal ganglia, which governs the off switch for thoughts and behaviors. . . .

Most anxiety disorders tend to skew female. Not so for OCD. Men make up 50 percent of the OCD population and, like me, they tend to develop symptoms earlier in life than women do. And given men's propensity to deny mental disorders, the numbers are probably higher.

But obsessions don't control me anymore. Thanks to chemistry, I've evicted the gnome who forever walked the same path in my mind. The rut he wore has grown over, and my attention no longer sinks into his steps. Still, I've carefully husbanded the obsessive-compulsive traits I like—just enough perfectionism on just the right things, plus a healthy dose of anxiety about my performance and how it is viewed. I rely on them to this day.

# Periodical Bibliography

*The following articles have been selected to supplement the diverse views presented in this chapter.*

Alicia Ault
"Most PTSD Therapies Not Supported by Evidence," *Internal Medicine News*, November 15, 2007.

Angela Bischoff
"Sounding the Pharma Alarm," *Briar Patch*, September-October 2007.

Michael J. Crumb
"Benefit of Time-Out Rooms Is Questioned: Experts See the Isolation Technique As Counterproductive, Especially for Students with Behavioral Disorders," *Los Angeles Times*, November 2, 2008.

Bruce Jancin
"PTSD Prevalence Justifies Screening of Injured Patients: At One Year, 1 in 5 Patients Meet Criteria," *Family Practice News*, May 15, 2008.

Martin L. Kutscher
"ADHD: Misconceptions and the Four Rules of Treatment," *Exceptional Parent*, September 2008.

Gary N. McAbee
"Benefits of ADHD Drugs May Trump Concerns Over Potential Risks," *AAP News*, June 2007.

Damian McNamara
"Parenting Is Crux of the Cure in Defiant Disorder," *Clinical Psychiatry News*, May 2008.

Gerald K. McOscar
"ADHD," Ifeminists.com, May 24, 2006.

Nancy Shute
"Skip the Ritalin and Treat Parents Instead," *U.S. News & World Report*, September 29, 2008.

Simon Wessely
"Can Talking Make You Better?" *New Statesman*, May 5, 2008.

CHAPTER 4

# What Policies Will Best Address the Challenges of Behavioral Disorders?

# Chapter Preface

During his twenty-one years in the Marine Corps, Jeff Johnson saw young adults walk into his recruiting office and walk out of boot camp as marines. Now, working at the Wisconsin Department of Veterans Affairs, Johnson claims that he sees something quite different in those coming back from Iraq and Afghanistan. Service members are being arrested for domestic violence, assault, and reckless and drunk driving. "The changes were dramatic. I'd never seen these kinds of changes in people," Johnson maintains. Indeed, between 2003 and 2007, the military diagnosed some 40,000 cases of post-traumatic stress disorder (PTSD) among troops deployed to Iraq and Afghanistan. Some estimates are even higher, and many mental health experts expect the trend to continue. Whether money will best solve the behavioral problems facing America's veterans and how to allocate these funds remains passionately contested.

Some believe that money is not enough. These analysts argue that war strategists need to reconsider the nature of the war being fought in Iraq and Afghanistan. According to sociologist David Segal at the University of Maryland's Center for Research on Military Organization, "There has to be a change in our thinking about what is going on in Afghanistan and Iraq. There has been an unwillingness to admit the number of psychological casualties coming out of this war." The troops in these countries are encountering unique conditions. "In past conflicts, there were tremendous differences in exposure to psychological trauma between combat troops and support troops. Now, it doesn't matter. . . . Basically, once you put boots on the ground in Iraq, you're in a combat zone," Segal argues.

Other commentators claim that funding is nonetheless the solution. According to Senate Veterans Affairs Committee chairman and World War II veteran Daniel K. Akaka, "Veterans are coming home with PTSD and other invisible wounds like TBI [traumatic brain injury], and the VA [Veterans Administration] should have been prepared for them, but they are not." Akaka has called for mandatory funding for VA health care, or at the very least, funding independent of annual congressional appropriations. Veterans' affairs activists agree. "If funding were mandatory," says L. Tammy Duckworth, herself a wounded Iraq-war veteran and director of Illinois' Department of Veterans Affairs, "every veteran who has a service-connected disability would have the care that this country promised them. That is what the American people think they're getting." House Veterans Affairs chairman Bob Filner thinks the simplicity of mandatory funding would also save money: "We'd be saving so much on bureaucracy. . . . They fought for us, they're ill, let's treat them."

Opponents believe that mandatory funding is fiscally irresponsible. Mandatory funding, they argue, discourages program improvements and efficiency. "I think it would be very bad judgment and bad policy to take advantage of the American people's compassion toward our wounded warriors," claims Representative Steve Buyer. Former senator Larry E. Craig agrees: "We already have three very large programs that are considered to be funded by 'mandatory spending'—namely Social Security, Medicare and Medicaid."

How best to address the behavioral disorders common among those suffering from the mental challenges of returning to civilian life after serving in Iraq and Afghanistan continues to be contested by mental health experts, veterans, and policy makers. The authors in the following chapter express their views on the policies that will successfully address behavioral disorders and their treatment.

> "[The vaccine court's Hannah Poling case] was a vindication for families who have been battling with the vaccine community, arguing that some poorly understood reaction to components of vaccines . . . could cause brain injury."

# The Vaccine Injury Compensation Program Gives Hope to Parents of Children with Autism

*Bernadine Healy*

*The Hannah Poling case, in which the vaccine court concluded that vaccines led to Hannah's autistic behavior, was a positive step for those parents who have long believed in the connection between vaccines and autism, maintains Bernadine Healy in the following viewpoint. Vaccines have historically been linked to neurological reactions, which led to a vaccine court. Despite claims by traditional medical organizations that there is no vaccine–autism link, she reasons that the case offers hope for those who disagree. Healy is a cardiologist and health policy analyst.*

As you read, consider the following questions:

1. According to Healy, why do some dismiss Hannah Poling as an anomaly?

2. What does the author think is the problem with population studies of vaccines?

3. In the author's opinion, what calls into question the universal vaccination strategy?

One of the most vitriolic debates in medical history is just beginning to have its day in court—vaccine court, that is. Without laying blame, the independent Office of Special Masters of the Court of Federal Claims—with a 20-year record of handling vaccine matters—recently conceded that the brain damage and autistic behavior of Hannah Poling stemmed from her exposure as a toddler to five vaccinations on one day in July 2000. Two days later, she was overtaken by a high fever and an encephalopathy that deteriorated into autistic behavior. Even though autism has a strong genetic basis, and she has a coexisting rare mitochondrial disorder, I would not be too quick to dismiss Hannah as an anomaly.

At some level, the decision was a vindication for families who have been battling with the vaccine community, arguing that some poorly understood reaction to components of vaccines or their mercury-based preservative, thimerosal, could cause brain injury. Yes, vaccines are extraordinarily safe and bring huge public health benefit. (Remember the 1950s polio epidemics?) But vaccine experts tend to look at the population as a whole, not at individual patients. And population studies are not granular enough to detect individual metabolic, genetic, or immunological variation that might make some children under certain circumstances susceptible to neurological complications after vaccination.

# A Trigger?

Families are not alone in searching for a trigger that might explain why autism and autism spectrum disorders have skyrocketed; now they reportedly affect about 1 in 150 kids. No doubt some of the increase is soft, due to broader diagnostic criteria, greater awareness, and—now that the notion of a detached "refrigerator" mom as a cause has blessedly fallen by the wayside—greater openness. But the rise of this disorder, which shows up before age 3, happens to coincide with the increased number and type of vaccine shots in the first few years of life. So as a trigger, vaccines carry a ring of both historical and biological plausibility.

Go back 40 or 50 years. The medical literature is replete with reports of neurological reactions to vaccines, such as mood changes, seizures, brain inflammation, and swelling. Several hundred cases of the paralytic illness Guillain-Barré after the swine flu vaccine were blamed on the government and gave [former president] Gerald Ford heartburn—but eventually led to the vaccine court.

Pediatricians were concerned enough about mercury, which is known to cause neurological damage in developing infant and fetal brains, that they mobilized to have thimerosal removed from childhood vaccines by 2002. Their concern was not autism but the lunacy of injecting mercury into little kids through mandated vaccines that together exceeded mercury safety guidelines designed for adults. But as in all things vaccine, this move too was contentious. Both the Centers for Disease Control and Prevention and the World Health Organization remain unconvinced that thimerosal puts young children at risk.

# A Need for More Research

There is no evidence that removal of thimerosal from vaccines has lowered autism rates. But autism numbers are not precise,

## What Is the Vaccine Court?

Formally known as the Office of Special Masters of the U.S. Court of Federal Claims, the vaccine court was set up to help people injured by inoculations while at the same time protecting manufacturers and doctors from crippling lawsuits. Eight judges, known as Special Masters, travel the country to hear cases. "I have had trials in people's living rooms because they couldn't go out with their brain-damaged child," says Chief Special Master Gary Golkiewicz. Since 1990 the court has compensated 944 petitioners.

*Sharon Cotliar,*
*"Autism & Vaccines: One Family's Victory,"*
People, *March 24, 2008.*

so I would say that considerably more research is still needed on some provocative findings. After all, thimerosal crosses the placenta, and pregnant women are advised to get flu shots, which often contain it. Studies in mice suggest that genetic variation influences brain sensitivity to the toxic effects of mercury. And a primate study designed to mimic vaccination in infants reported in 2005 that thimerosal may clear from the blood in a matter of days but leaves inorganic mercury behind in the brain.

The debate roils on—even about research. The Institute of Medicine [IOM] in its last report on vaccines and autism in 2004 said that more research on the vaccine question is counterproductive: Finding a susceptibility to this risk in some infants would call into question the universal vaccination strategy that is a bedrock of immunization programs and could lead to widespread rejection of vaccines. The IOM concluded that efforts to find a link between vaccines and autism "must be balanced against the broader benefit of the current vaccine program for all children."

Wow. Medicine has moved ahead only because doctors, researchers, and yes, families, have openly challenged even the most sacred medical dogma. At the risk of incurring the wrath of some of my dearest colleagues, I say thank goodness for the vaccine court.

> *"The message that the [Vaccine Injury Compensation Program] inadvertently sends to the public will further erode confidence in vaccines and hurt those whom it is charged with protecting."*

# The Vaccine Injury Compensation Program Is Unfair and Dangerous

*Paul A. Offit*

*In the following viewpoint, Paul A. Offit argues that by concluding that vaccines cause autism absent any evidence to support the claim, the Vaccine Injury Compensation Program (VICP), also known as the vaccine court, has turned its back on science. Established to compensate families who suffer vaccine-related damages, the court also protects pharmaceutical companies from specious claims, he explains. Allowing compensation absent evidence erodes public confidence in the vaccines that protect them, he reasons. Dr. Offit is chief of infectious diseases at the Children's Hospital of Philadelphia and professor of pediatrics at the University of Pennsylania School of Medicine—both in Philadelphia.*

As you read, consider the following questions:

1. In Offit's view, what case represents a great deviation from the VICP's original standards?

2. According to the author, how many immunologic components do today's vaccines contain?

3. What, in Offit's view, is evident in all children with profound impairments in cognition?

On April 11, 2008, the National Vaccine Advisory Committee took an unusual step: in the name of transparency, trust, and collaboration, it asked members of the public to help set its vaccine-safety research agenda for the next 5 years. Several parents, given this opportunity, expressed concern that vaccines might cause autism—a fear that had recently been fueled by extensive media coverage of a press conference involving a 9-year-old girl named Hannah Poling.

When she was 19 months old, Hannah, the daughter of Jon and Terry Poling, received five vaccines: diphtheria-tetanus-acellular pertussis, *Haemophilus influenzae* type b (Hib), measles-mumps-rubella (MMR), varicella, and inactivated polio. At the time, Hannah was interactive, playful, and communicative. Two days later, she was lethargic, irritable, and febrile. Ten days after vaccination, she developed a rash consistent with vaccine-induced varicella.

Months later, with delays in neurologic and psychological development, Hannah was diagnosed with encephalopathy caused by a mitochondrial enzyme deficit. Hannah's signs included problems with language, communication, and behavior—all features of autism spectrum disorder. Although it is not unusual for children with mitochondrial enzyme deficiencies to develop neurologic signs between their first and second years of life, Hannah's parents believed that vaccines had triggered her encephalopathy. They sued the Department of

Health and Human Services (DHHS) for compensation under the Vaccine Injury Compensation Program (VICP) and won.

On March 6, 2008, the Polings took their case to the public. Standing before a bank of microphones from several major news organizations, Jon Poling said that "the results in this case may well signify a landmark decision with children developing autism following vaccinations."[1] For years, federal health agencies and professional organizations had reassured the public that vaccines didn't cause autism. Now, with DHHS making this concession in a federal claims court, the government appeared to be saying exactly the opposite. Caught in the middle, clinicians were at a loss to explain the reasoning behind the VICP's decision.

The Poling case is best understood in the context of the decision-making process of this unusual vaccine court. In the late 1970s and early 1980s, American lawyers successfully sued pharmaceutical companies claiming that vaccines caused a variety of illnesses, including unexplained coma, sudden infant death syndrome, Reye's syndrome, transverse myelitis, mental retardation, and epilepsy. By 1986, all but one manufacturer of the diphtheria-tetanus-pertussis vaccine had left the market. The federal government stepped in, passing the National Childhood Vaccine Injury Act, which included the creation of the VICP. Funded by a federal excise tax on each dose of vaccine, the VICP compiled a list of compensable injuries. If scientific studies supported the notion that vaccines caused an adverse event—such as thrombocytopenia after receipt of measles-containing vaccine or paralysis after receipt of oral polio vaccine—children and their families were compensated quickly, generously, and fairly. The number of lawsuits against vaccine makers decreased dramatically.

Unfortunately, in recent years the VICP seems to have turned its back on science. In 2005, Margaret Althen successfully claimed that a tetanus vaccine had caused her optic neuritis. Although there was no evidence to support her claim,

> ## The Vaccine Court Will Not End the Debate
>
> As a parent of a child with autism, . . . I base my opinion on scientific literature and no court decision is going to change it. Neither will a court decision change the minds of the antivaccine advocates. Two distinct communities have emerged, and though they both employ the language of science, their ideas are simply incommensurable. The two groups co-exist, like creationism and evolutionary biology, but they operate on such different premises that a true dialogue is nearly impossible.
>
> *Roy Richard Grinker, "Science on Trial,"*
> Wall Street Journal, *June 30, 2007.*

the VICP ruled that if a petitioner proposed a biologically plausible mechanism by which a vaccine could cause harm, as well as a logical sequence of cause and effect, an award should be granted. The door opened by this and other rulings allowed petitioners to claim successfully that the MMR vaccine caused fibromyalgia and epilepsy, the hepatitis B vaccine caused Guillain-Barré syndrome and chronic demyelinating polyneuropathy, and the Hib vaccine caused transverse myelitis.

No case, however, represented a greater deviation from the VICP's original standards than that of Dorothy Werderitsh, who in 2006 successfully claimed that a hepatitis B vaccine had caused her multiple sclerosis. By the time of the ruling, several studies had shown that hepatitis B vaccine neither caused nor exacerbated the disease, and the Institute of Medicine had concluded that "evidence favors rejection of a causal relationship between hepatitis B vaccine and multiple sclerosis."[2] But the VICP was less impressed with the scientific literature than it was with an expert's proposal of a mechanism by which hepatitis B vaccine could induce autoimmunity (an ironic conclusion, given that Dorothy Werderitsh never had a detectable immune response to the vaccine).

Like the Werderitsh decision, the VICP's concession to Hannah Poling was poorly reasoned. First, whereas it is clear that natural infections can exacerbate symptoms of encephalopathy in patients with mitochondrial enzyme deficiencies, no clear evidence exists that vaccines cause similar exacerbations. Indeed, because children with such deficiencies are particularly susceptible to infections, it is recommended that they receive all vaccines.

Second, the belief that the administration of multiple vaccines can overwhelm or weaken the immune system of a susceptible child is at variance with the number of immunologic components contained in modern vaccines. A century ago, children received one vaccine, smallpox, which contained about 200 structural and nonstructural viral proteins. Today, thanks to advances in protein purification and recombinant DNA technology, the 14 vaccines given to young children contain a total of about 150 immunologic components.[3]

Third, although experts testifying on behalf of the Polings could reasonably argue that development of fever and a varicella-vaccine rash after the administration of nine vaccines was enough to stress a child with mitochondrial enzyme deficiency, Hannah had other immunologic challenges that were not related to vaccines. She had frequent episodes of fever and otitis media, eventually necessitating placement of bilateral polyethylene tubes. Nor is such a medical history unusual. Children typically have four to six febrile illnesses each year during their first few years of life[4]; vaccines are a minuscule contributor to this antigenic challenge.

Fourth, without data that clearly exonerate vaccines, it could be argued that children with mitochondrial enzyme deficiencies might have a lower risk of exacerbations if vaccines were withheld, delayed, or separated. But such changes would come at a price. Even spacing out vaccinations would increase the period during which children were susceptible to natural infections, giving a theoretical risk from vaccines priority over a known risk from vaccine-preventable diseases. These diseases aren't merely historical: pneumococcus, varicella, and pertussis are still common in the United States. Recent measles outbreaks in California, Arizona, and Wisconsin among children whose parents had chosen not to vaccinate them show the real risks of public distrust of immunization.

After the Polings' press conference, Julie Gerberding, director of the Centers for Disease Control and Prevention, responded to their claims that vaccines had caused their daughter's autism. "Let me be very clear that the government has made absolutely no statement . . . indicating that vaccines are a cause of autism," she said.[5] Gerberding's biggest challenge was defining the term "autism." Because autism is a clinical diagnosis, children are labeled as autistic on the basis of a collection of clinical features. Hannah Poling clearly had difficulties with language, speech, and communication. But those features of her condition considered autistic were part of a global encephalopathy caused by a mitochondrial enzyme deficit. Rett's syndrome, tuberous sclerosis, fragile X syndrome, and Down's syndrome in children can also have autistic features. Indeed, features reminiscent of autism are evident in all children with profound impairments in cognition; but these similarities are superficial, and their causal mechanisms and genetic influences are different from those of classic autism.

Going forward, the VICP should more rigorously define the criteria by which it determines that a vaccine has caused harm. Otherwise, the message that the program inadvertently sends to the public will further erode confidence in vaccines and hurt those whom it is charged with protecting.

Dr. Offit reports being a co-inventor and co-holder of a patent on the rotavirus vaccine RotaTeq, from which he and his institution receive royalties, as well as serving on a scientific advisory board for Merck. No other potential conflict of interest relevant to this article was reported.

# Notes

1. CNN. American Morning. March 6, 2008 (television broadcast).
2. Stratton K, Almario DA, McCormick MC, eds. Immunization safety review: hepatitis B vaccine and demyelinating neurological disorders. Washington, DC: National Academies Press, 2002.
3. Offit PA, Quarles J, Gerber MA, et al. Addressing parents' concerns: do multiple vaccines overwhelm or weaken the infant's immune system? Pediatrics 2002;109:124-129.
4. Dingle JH, Badger GF, Jordan WS Jr. Illness in the home: a study of 25,000 illnesses in a group of Cleveland families. Cleveland: Press of Western Reserve University, 1964.
5. Rovner J. Case stokes debate about autism, vaccines. National Public Radio (NPR), March 7, 2008. (Available at http://www.npr.org/templates/story/story.php?storyId= 87974932.)

> *"Pleasantville's autism program is very well regarded, enough so that it was recently listed as a selling point in a real estate ad for a high priced house."*

# Mainstreaming Benefits Autistic Students

*Leslie Werstein Hann*

*In the following viewpoint, Leslie Werstein Hann claims that autistic students benefit from mainstreaming. While every child with autism is different, the trend has been to have them learn in the same environment as their peers, rather than a special school. Hann uses the Pleasantville Union Free School District as an example of autistic students succeeding in a program that uses mainstreaming. Leslie Werstein Hann is a freelance writer and contributor to* District Administration.

As you read, consider the following questions:

1. According to data released by the U.S. Centers for Disease Control, about 1 child in how many has autism?

2. How much was the Pleasantville Union Free School District paying to educate each autistic student at an out-of-district program?

Leslie Werstein Hann, "Addressing Autism," *District Administration*, October 2007, pp. 43–51. Copyright © 2007 Professional Media Group LLC. Reproduced by permission.

3. What are some of the keys to success for the Pleasantville Union Free School District's autism program?

As the fastest growing developmental disability, autism presents one of the greatest special education challenges facing school districts today. In February, the U.S. Centers for Disease Control released data showing that about 1 child in 150 has a form of autism, when previous estimates put the figure at 4 or 5 per 10,000. According to the U.S. Department of Education, the number of children age 3 to 21 in federally supported programs for autism increased from 22,000 in the 1993–1994 school year to 223,000 in 2005–2006.

Autism is a complex brain disorder characterized by difficulties interacting with people and communicating verbally and nonverbally. People with autism also exhibit repetitive behaviors and interests, and they may have unusual responses to sensory experiences, such as the way something looks or sounds. The barely audible buzz of a fluorescent light just beginning to flicker might cause ear-splitting pain for a child with autism. Its various forms, including Asperger syndrome and autistic disorder, are known broadly as autism spectrum disorders (ASD), though autism is often used as an umbrella term.

Among the most important characteristics of autism, and one that creates a great challenge for schools, is that it is so different for every person. While there are specific techniques that are known to be effective, one teaching methodology is not appropriate for all children with ASD. In addition, children with autism require services at home and in the community to help them "generalize" what they learn in school to other settings. Children with ASD may also need speech, occupational, behavioral and other therapies.

## Pleasantville Union Free School District

The Pleasantville Union Free School District in Westchester County, N.Y., always had a reputation for providing high quality special education services, especially for children with learning disabilities. Until a few years ago, however, the district was incapable of serving its growing population of children with autism-related disorders. Like many small districts, Pleasantville, which serves 1,800 K12 students, was paying mightily—well over $65,000 in tuition, transportation and other service costs—to educate each student with autism at an out-of-district program run by the local educational services cooperative, BOCES, or Board of Cooperative Educational Services.

But parents began insisting that their children be able to attend the local school, especially since many of them were doing well in mainstream preschool classes with the support of a special education teacher. The Individuals with Disabilities Education Act requires schools to provide a free, appropriate education in the "least restrictive environment," so Pleasantville district leaders gave it a try. The program started in 2003 with two children; the following year, four more autistic children entered kindergarten at Bedford Road School, the district's elementary school.

Pleasantville uses three models—full mainstreaming with classroom aides, pullouts for direct instruction, and self-contained classrooms—to educate more than 15 children in the elementary school. The district hired a specialist to work with families and another teacher to support close to 10 children with autism in its middle and high schools, providing direct instruction for those who need it. Older students also receive job coaching and community-based instruction, an important but often overlooked component to help them transition into life after high school.

Now three years later, Pleasantville's autism program is very well regarded, enough so that it was recently listed as a selling point in a real estate ad for a high priced house. Key elements of the district's success include its willingness to

## A Mainstreaming Chronology

1975: Congress requires free and appropriate public education for all children with disabilities, which is later named the Individuals with Disabilities Education Act (IDEA).

1982: The Supreme Court holds in *Board of Education of the Hendrick Hudson School District v. Rowley* that the purpose of the IDEA law is to provide appropriate but not optimal special education.

1988: A federal court holds in *Polk v. Central Susquehanna Intermediate Unit 16* that IDEA requires states to provide more than a minimal education to disabled children, which opens the door to lawsuits for more expensive programs.

1991: The Department of Education adds autism as a category eligible for free special-education services.

*Compiled by editor.*

budget for experienced staff and the flexibility to adapt the program to the changing needs of the individual children being served.

"We have demonstrated that not only have we ended up providing a higher quality of education," says Carolyn McGuffog, the district's director of educational services, "but we are doing it at a substantial cost savings for the district.

"I'm very proud of what we're doing," McGuffog adds, "but I'm anxious for other districts to do it too."

## Mainstreaming Trend

While some children with autism attend special schools—both public and private—the prevailing winds are definitely blowing in the other direction. "There are and have been special schools for autism because the behaviors can be so challenging and there's such a great push for specialized approaches," says Linda Hickson, director of the Center for Opportunities and Outcomes for People with Disabilities at Columbia University's Teachers College in New York. "But the trend is toward serving more children in-district, and the challenge for district administrators is finding how best to serve children in their regular schools so they can be there with their peers."

The decision on when a child is best served in the home district or outside depends on the circumstance. "My question in every meeting with parents and teachers is, What are the child's characteristics? What does he or she need to learn, and where can the child best be taught that information?" says Brenda Smith Myles, chief of programs and development at the Ohio Center for Autism and Low Incidence, a federally funded information clearinghouse under the Ohio Department of Education, Office for Exceptional Children. "In most cases, public schools should be able to provide that."

> "[A disabled child's] preschool class-mates rarely played with him and he came home from summer camp asking why the nondisabled children laughed at him."

# Mainstreaming Can Hinder Autistic Students

*Robert Tomsho*

*Mainstreaming often does autistic children more harm than good, claims Robert Tomsho in the following viewpoint. He reports that the parents of these children claim that separate special-education schools would provide their autistic children with a better education. Unfortunately, in budget-strapped states, these schools are threatened. Advocates argue, however, that publicly funded special schools are actually more cost-effective. Moreover, Tomsho discusses how many parents contend that their children should not be mainstreamed simply to promote an ideology of inclusion. Tomsho is a staff writer for the* Wall Street Journal.

As you read, consider the following questions:

1. In Tomsho's view, why do legislators often side with mainstreaming advocates?

2. According to the author, which state was one of the first to pass special-education laws?

3. According to Mark Finkelstein, what convinced county officials in the Monroe Township of New Jersey to back bonds for special-education schools?

[In the fall of 2006], groups who favor placing disabled students in regular classrooms faced opposition from an unlikely quarter: parents like Norette Travis, whose daughter Valerie has autism.

## A Growing Group

Valerie had already tried the mainstreaming approach that the disability-advocacy groups were supporting. After attending a preschool program for special-needs students, she was assigned to a regular kindergarten class. But there, her mother says, she disrupted class, ran through the hallways and lashed out at others—at one point giving a teacher a black eye.

"She did not learn anything that year," Ms. Travis recalls. "She regressed."

As policy makers push to include more special-education students into general classrooms, factions are increasingly divided. Advocates for the disabled say special-education students benefit both academically and socially by being taught alongside typical students. Legislators often side with them, arguing that mainstreaming is productive for students and cost-effective for taxpayers.

Some teachers and administrators have been less supportive of the practice, saying that they lack the training and resources to handle significantly disabled children. And more parents are joining the dissenters. People like Ms. Travis believe that mainstreaming can actually hinder the students it is intended to help. Waging a battle to preserve older policies, these parents are demanding segregated teaching environments—including separate schools.

## The Goal of Integration

In 2005, more than half of all special-education students were considered mainstreamed, or "fully included," nationally. These students spent 80% or more of the school day in regular classrooms, up from about a third in 1990, according to the U.S. Department of Education.

"The burden is on school districts and states to give strong justification for why a child or group of children cannot be integrated," says Thomas Hehir, an education professor at Harvard and former director of special education at the U.S. Department of Education.

That point of view frustrates many parents. Some have struggled to get services from their local school districts; others have seen their disabled children falter in integrated settings.

Mary Kaplowitz, a special-education teacher in Kingston, Pa., was a bigger supporter of mainstreaming before she had her son, Zachary, who has autism and is mildly retarded. She says his preschool classmates rarely played with him and he came home from summer camp asking why the nondisabled children laughed at him. On a visit, she saw them drawing away from her son.

"They shunned him and it broke my heart," says Ms. Kaplowitz. Earlier this year [in 2007], she and other parents fought successfully to preserve separate special-education classes in Kingston like the one Zachary, now 9 years old, attends at a local elementary school.

## Separate Schools

Such parental pushback has prompted local school districts across the country to delay or downsize mainstreaming initiatives.

[In 2006], parents of disabled kids in Walworth County, Wis., clashed with an advocacy group over the creation of a new special-education school. As part of the battle, Disability Rights Wisconsin sued the county in Milwaukee federal court to try to block the school. The new school is currently under construction and the lawsuit is under appeal.

And earlier this year [in 2007], parents in Maryland's Montgomery County asked the state to continue a special-education program their school district was scheduled to discontinue. After initial protests, the district agreed to phase out the program—letting enrolled kids continue—rather than close it outright.

The debate has grown contentious in New Jersey, a state with a strong tradition of separate education for the disabled. Only about 41% of the state's 230,000 special-education students are deemed fully included, compared with 54% nationwide. About 9% of the state's disabled students—triple the national average—attend separate schools.

New Jersey passed some of the nation's first special-education laws. In the 1950s, it began requiring public schools to pay for special-ed services that they didn't offer. State law also gave counties and groups of school districts broad powers to build stand-alone schools for the disabled. Today, there are 80 publicly funded separate schools for the disabled in New Jersey and about 175 private ones. They receive tuition from public districts for handling special-ed students.

## Costs Are a Barrier

But in 2004, the state, which had faced federal pressure to mainstream, placed a year-long moratorium on the opening of new special-education schools. Since then, it has stiffened the approval process for private facilities and bolstered funding for local districts to broaden in-house programs.

In a budget-strapped state where voters have been demanding tax relief, cost has been a factor. On average, New

## A Need for Flexibility

We need to have flexibility in policies, recognizing that there are different kinds of special needs students with different kinds of special needs. Policies that rigidly maintain ideological values may be harmful.

We should be able to offer mainstreaming and segregation options.

*Anton Miller,*
*"Special Needs Debate Doesn't Need Ideology,"*
Vancouver Sun, *March 5, 2007.*

Jersey spends about $16,100 a year on each special-education student, including those who are mainstreamed. The average annual tuition at the various, separate public schools for the disabled range from $28,500 to $42,000; at private schools, it's $44,000.

Overall, tuition and transportation costs for out-of-district placements accounted for 39% of the $3.3 billion a year that the state spends on special education. "That's a huge cost driver for our education budget," says state Sen. John Adler, who last year co-chaired hearings on school funding reform.

Many parents, including state Sen. Stephen Sweeney, bristle at moves that could foreclose their options. His daughter, Lauren, who has Down syndrome, attends a regular middle school. But Mr. Sweeney says her nondisabled classmates never visit or ask her to hang out. Next year, he's moving Lauren to a separate high school operated by the publicly funded Gloucester County Special Services School District. The system's special-education facilities also include a new $14 million school for children with autism and multiple disabilities.

## The Choice of Parents

"Just to put my child in a building to make people feel better because it's inclusion is outrageous," says Mr. Sweeney. "As long as I am in the legislature, they are not going to take away the choice of parents with children with disabilities."

The school funding hearings, held in various towns and cities last fall, were emotional. Ruth Lowenkron, a special-education attorney, testified that beyond being the right thing to do, mainstreaming would save money. "Repeat after me," she told the legislators, "inclusion is cheaper than segregation."

But the panel also heard often from parents who argued for continued access to separate schools.

They included Adela Maria Bolet, of Teaneck, N.J., whose suit-clad son, Michael, sat beside his mother while she testified. The 17-year-old, who has Down syndrome, now attends a private high school on the state's tab. In earlier years, Ms. Bolet fought to get Michael into regular public schools only to find that he sometimes became depressed and had little positive interaction with nondisabled peers.

Until high school, he had few friends, says Ms. Bolet. Her voice still quivers when she talks about what happened when the family rented a pool in town and invited classmates from Michael's neighborhood elementary school to a swimming party for his 13th birthday. "Nobody came," she says.

## School Resources

Concurrent with the funding hearings, another debate was boiling at New Jersey's publicly funded Middlesex Regional Education Services Commission. It had already supported and built a network of six special-education schools, and planned to open two more, including a 24-classroom facility. The commission, controlled by a consortium of school districts, had built its other schools using bonds guaranteed by Middlesex County's governing board. Its school projects had never faced significant opposition.

This time was different, as the proposed schools became a target for mainstreaming advocates. Critics like William England, a school board member in South River, N.J., wrote to local papers. To endorse the sort of segregated special-education schools that most of the country is busy abandoning would be "a waste of county resources," he said in a letter to the *Home News Tribune*, East Brunswick, N.J.

Mark Finkelstein, the Middlesex commission's superintendent, scoffs at such criticism. He estimates his schools save local districts $10 million a year over the cost of placement in privately owned facilities. "It's easy to say that all kids should be in mainstream schools but let's talk reality," he says.

On a recent morning at the Bright Beginnings Learning Center—one of the Middlesex schools—a hallway painted mint-green was lined with children's wheelchairs and walkers. In one classroom, a teacher and four aides were working with seven disabled students, most strapped into devices designed to help them stand or sit.

Mary Lou Walker, an aide, crouched beside the desk of Teresa Condora, a petite 7-year-old who suffers from cerebral palsy and is largely nonverbal. "All right T, come on," Ms. Walker said, gently urging the girl to press a big red plastic button attached to a buzzer. Responding with a soft moan, Teresa pushed against the button as though it were impossibly heavy.

## Factions Face Off

Last September, pro- and anti-mainstreaming factions faced off at a meeting where the fate of the proposed new Middlesex schools was to be decided.

At the microphone that evening, Paula Lieb, president of the New Jersey Coalition for Inclusive Education, cited multiple examples of severely disabled children who had been successfully mainstreamed. She said that "the vast majority of children can be included in the public schools."

But the parents of children already attending the commission's schools had also been organizing, urging each other to come to the hearing and bring their disabled children.

Sandy Epstein's family had moved to New Jersey from Oregon a decade earlier to take advantage of specialized schools for students like her son, Brandon, who has autism. For the hearing, the 48-year-old homemaker dressed her teenager in a bright red polo shirt and sat near the front. "I wanted him to stand out," she says. "I wanted these politicians to see what we are talking about."

Ms. Travis, a 41-year-old bookkeeper from Milltown, N.J., says that while waiting to speak that night, she grew angry with the criticisms of the inclusion advocates. She thought they had no idea what her daughter Valerie, now 11, needed.

The Travises had spent eight months on a waiting list to get Valerie into the Academy Learning Center, one of the Middlesex schools located in Monroe Township, N.J.

During that time, she says, the progress Valerie had made learning to speak all but disappeared. Along with reports of her outbursts at school, Ms. Travis says the family had to cope with frequent meltdowns at home. Valerie slept fitfully, ripped up her homework and beat up her little brother to the point that he once needed stitches.

"It was the worst eight months of our lives," Ms. Travis told the county officials, adding that families like hers needed schools like the Academy, where Valerie is now learning geography and double-digit subtraction.

Mr. Finkelstein believes parents' testimony helped convince county officials to unanimously back the bonds needed for the new construction, which is under way.

"If inclusion worked for all of our residents," the superintendent says, "they wouldn't be fighting so hard for these new schools."

Their efforts are far from over. In June [2007], a coalition of disability-rights groups sued the New Jersey education department in U.S. District Court in Newark. Taking a page from the racial desegregation battles of the 1960s, it alleges the department isn't moving fast enough to integrate disabled students and asks the federal court to take over the process.

> *"Some veterans and veterans' advocates have been vocal in their belief that personality disorder is being misdiagnosed in combat veterans."*

# Veterans Should Not Be Wrongly Discharged with Personality Disorder

### *Bob Woodruff, James Hill, Jaime Hennessey, and Joshua Kors*

*In the following viewpoint, Bob Woodruff, James Hill, Jaime Hennessey, and Joshua Kors argue that to avoid paying for post-traumatic stress disorder (PTSD) treatment, the U.S. military is unfairly discharging Iraq veterans with personality disorder. Since a personality disorder predates military service, the military asserts that these veterans are not entitled to medical care and disability payments. The authors report how veterans' advocates assert that the U.S. military should discontinue this shameful practice and keep its promise to those who suffer from combat-related PTSD. Woodruff, Hill, and Hennessey are* ABC News *journalists; Kors writes for the* Nation.

As you read, consider the following questions:

1. What was the nature of Army specialist Jonathan Town's injuries?

2. According to veterans' advocate Russell K. Terry, why did the military deploy thousands of soldiers with personality disorder?

3. What impact did musician Dave Matthews have on the personality disorder debate?

A rmy Specialist Jonathan Town is back home in Ohio now, but still very much at war.

"When you see bits and pieces of actual people or people bleeding to death or anything, it's very unsettling. It's something you'll never be able to forget. Period," Town told *ABC News'* Bob Woodruff.

Since his discharge in 2006, Town has not only dealt with the emotional scars of war, but he has also found himself at the center of a national debate on mental health care for veterans as a crowd as diverse as singer Dave Matthews and members of Congress has questioned how 22,000 veterans were diagnosed and discharged since 2001.

In Town's case, the discharge came two years after he was injured in an attack. In the fall of 2004, a 107 mm rocket ripped through his unit's headquarters in Ramadi, exploding two feet above Town's head and knocking him unconscious.

The rocket blast left Town with hearing loss, headaches, memory problems, anxiety and insomnia. For his wounds, he was awarded the Purple Heart.

But when he returned to the states seeking treatment for those very wounds, the Army quickly discharged him, asserting his problems had been caused not by the war but by a personality disorder that predated his military career.

## A Quick Way Out

It is known as a "Chapter 5-13": "separation because of personality disorder." The Army defines it as a pre-existing "maladaptive pattern of behavior of long duration" that interferes with the soldier's ability to perform his duties.

In practical terms, this diagnosis means the personality disorder existed before military service, and therefore medical care and disability payments are not the military's responsibility. But some veterans and veterans' advocates have been vocal in their belief that personality disorder is being misdiagnosed in combat veterans.

"A significant percentage of the ones who are discharged with personality disorder truly have it, but there is another percentage that are put out simply to eliminate them from military service. . . . It's done maliciously or as some sort of a policy," said Russell K. Terry, founder of the veterans' advocacy organization, Iraq War Veterans Organization.

Since 2001, more than 22,000 servicemen and women from all branches of the military have been separated under the personality disorder discharge, according to figures provided by the Department of Defense.

The military explained the need for this kind of discharge. "Personality disorders that interfere with military service and are incompatible with the soldier staying in the unit, it is usually best for both the soldier and the unit for that soldier to be discharged," according to Colonel Elspeth Cameron Ritchie, a psychiatry consultant to the U.S. Army surgeon general.

Servicemen and women undergo mental and physical screenings when they enter the military and again before they deploy. "Either the military didn't see it or they ignored it," Terry said.

"We do histories and physicals on every recruit that comes in, but people may not always tell us everything," Ritchie said.

## The Veterans' Perspective

Donald Louis Schmidt of Chillicothe, Ill., was being treated for posttraumatic stress disorder after his second combat tour in Iraq. His commanders at Fort Carson later decided he was no longer mentally fit and discharged him with personality disorder.

"They just slapped me with that label to get me out quicker," Schmidt said. He said superiors told him "'Everything will be great. Peachy keen.' Well, it's not."

The discharge left Schmidt ineligible for disability pay and benefits. He was also required to return more than $10,000 of his $15,000 reenlistment bonus, but he said no one explained that to him until it was too late.

"If I didn't have family, I'd be living on the sidewalk," Schmidt said.

"It's not right that they would do this to him after him going to war for us," Schmidt's mother, Patrice Semtner-Myers, said. "They threw him away. They're done with him. He's no use to them anymore so they say, 'We're done. . . . Thanks for nothing.'"

Schmidt and Town say Army doctors misled them about the consequences of the personality disorder discharge. Town said he was told he would receive his benefits and it would be like a medical discharge, only quicker.

In the course of reporting this story, *ABC News* spoke with 20 Iraq War veterans who believe they were misdiagnosed with personality disorder.

A Marine who preferred not to be named said, "Most docs won't diagnose you with PTSD [posttraumatic stress disorder] because the military has to treat you for the rest of your life."

After confrontations with his commander, Private First Class David Vann said a psychologist met with him for "10 minutes and said, 'I think you're lying about PTSD. . . . I think you have [personality disorder].'"

"If they cared about my well-being, they would have tried to fix it. The Army would rather [sever] all the ties," Army Specialist William Wooldridge said.

The military would not comment on specific cases. Ritchi said, "If there was a mistake that was made, and we're a big organization, it is possible that mistakes were made, that we have the ability to go back and relook at that diagnosis and that discharge."

## A Whistle-Blower

On the day he was discharged in the fall, Town met with Jeff Peskoff, a civilian employee in the personnel office at Fort Carson in Colorado, and learned he owed the Army $3,000 to repay his enlistment bonus.

"At some points it looked like he wanted to cry and at some point he looked like he wanted to rip my head off," Peskoff said.

Peskoff, who served 10 years in the Army, including a tour of Iraq, recently quit his job in disgust and is now speaking publicly for the first time.

"If you have a combat tour and you are getting labeled as a personality disorder, there is something wrong. It's a lie," Peskoff said. "It's a quick way to get rid of that body and bring in another body. And it's a quick way to save money."

In the span of several months, Peskoff said he processed the personality disorder discharges of Schmidt, Town and hundreds of other combat veterans he believed were actually suffering physical and psychological trauma because of the war.

"They [Army officials] are basically washing their hands of them," Peskoff said.

Fort Carson officials declined to talk to *ABC News* about this story. The Government Accountability Office is currently investigating Fort Carson as part of a larger study of mental health services for veterans.

## Taking Notice

Some prominent people took notice of Town's case after he was profiled in a *Nation* article earlier this year [2007]. Musician Dave Matthews spoke about him at a concert this spring at Radio City Music Hall in New York.

"Fans at the show started talking about it among themselves and then they started collecting money to support Jon Town," Matthews said.

The Dave Matthews Band collected 23,000 signatures on its fan site for a letter requesting that Congress and the Department of Defense look into the personality disorder discharges.

"They're forever changed," Matthews said. "We should look after these kids."

Town's story also inspired 31 senators, including four presidential candidates, to write to Defense Secretary Robert Gates calling for an investigation into the military's use of the personality disorder discharge.

"We are concerned over continuing reports from veterans' services organizations, the media and individual U.S. service personnel that personality disorder discharges have been implemented inappropriately and inconsistently," the letter said.

Sen. Kit Bond, R-Mo., said, "We want to make this something that is widely understood and gain the momentum for necessary changes to the system."

Just today [July 2007], six senators including Bond and Barack Obama, D-Illinois, introduced an amendment to the National Defense Authorization Act that would temporarily suspend personality disorder discharges for combat veterans until there is a comprehensive review of the current procedures.

Gates and other Defense Department officials declined to speak to *ABC News,* saying the issue was under review by the veteran care commission headed by Democrat Donna Shalala and Republican Bob Dole.

After all the recent attention focused on Town, the Department of Veterans Affairs recently began treating him and paying disability benefits.

Matthews was asked whether his actions had helped Town. "I think the push, the publicness of the whole thing had some bearing on that, and if it did, it's great that it did. But there are still a lot of other soldiers that need to have the same attention paid on their behalf."

At home in central Illinois, Donald Schmidt is waiting.

"*Diagnoses [of returning military veterans] reflect a personality disorder if present but, in my personal experience, this has been rare.*"

# The Number of Veterans Wrongly Discharged with Personality Disorder Is Exaggerated

*Tracie Shea*

*The symptoms of post-traumatic stress disorder (PTSD) and preexisting personality disorder (PD) have similar features and can even coexist in veterans exposed to combat, claims Tracie Shea in the following excerpt from testimony before the House Committee on Veterans' Affairs. Nevertheless, she argues, a personality disorder discharge following combat is rare. Once the onset of symptoms has been determined to be prior to military service, a diagnosis of PD should, in fact, be made and distinguished from PTSD. Shea is a psychologist at the Post Traumatic Stress Disorder Clinic at the Veterans Affairs Medical Center in Providence, Rhode Island.*

Tracie Shea, "Statement of Tracie Shea, Ph.D. Psychologist, Post Traumatic Stress Disorder Clinic Veterans Affairs Medical Center Providence, Rhode Island, Department of Veterans Affairs, before the House Committee on Veterans' Affairs," United States Department of Veterans Affairs, July 25, 2007.

As you read, consider the following questions:

1. According to Shea, how does the DSM-IV define personality disorder?

2. What does the author say can happen to a person who functions in spite of a mild to moderate personality disorder after experiencing trauma?

3. In the author's opinion, when should a clinical diagnosis of personality disorder be made?

I am honored at the opportunity to provide testimony to the Committee [on Veterans Affairs] on issues related to Post Traumatic Stress Disorder (PTSD) and Personality Disorders. . . .

I come before this Committee, not as a representative or spokesperson for the Department of Veterans Affairs (VA) but as a mental health researcher who has conducted extensive research on Personality Disorders. My thoughts and opinions, which I will share with you today, are my own and should not be taken as VA's views or policy.

As a psychologist on the clinical staff of the Post Traumatic Stress Disorder Clinic at the Veterans Affairs Medical Center [VAMC] in Providence, Rhode Island for the past 17 years, I have assessed and treated hundreds of veterans. I also conduct research on personality disorders and on PTSD as part of my academic role as professor of Psychiatry and Human Behavior at the Warren Alpert Medical School, Brown University. Of note to the topic of today's hearing, I was a member of the subcommittee responsible for the revision of the Personality Disorders section for the 4th edition of the *Diagnostic and Statistical Manual for Mental Disorders* (DSM-IV).

The Committee has requested my testimony regarding PTSD and Personality Disorders in the context of service members and veterans. My comments will focus on requirements set forth in VA and used at all VAMC facilities for an adequate assessment and diagnosis of personality disorder. With regard to the use of appropriate procedures, I will speak to my personal experience conducting assessments as a psychologist at the VA in Providence.

## The Definition of Personality Disorder

A Personality Disorder is defined by the DSM-IV [a comprehensive classification of officially recognized psychiatric disorders] as an enduring pattern of inner experience and behavior that deviates markedly from the expectations of the individual's culture, manifested in cognition (ways of perceiving or interpreting events, others' behavior), affect (range, intensity, lability, appropriateness of emotional response), interpersonal functioning, or impulse control. For a diagnosis to be made, several requirements must be met:

1. The enduring pattern is inflexible and pervasive across a broad range of personal and social situations. This means that problematic behaviors should be evident in multiple situations.

2. The pattern of behavior is stable and of long duration, and its onset can be traced back at least to adolescence or early adulthood.

3. There is evidence of significant distress or impairment in functioning associated with the enduring pattern of behavior.

4. The pattern of behavior is not better accounted for as a manifestation or consequence of another mental disorder

5. The pattern is not due to the direct physiological effects of a substance (e.g. a drug of abuse, a medication) or a general medical condition (e.g. head trauma).

# Distinguishing Between Personality Disorder and PTSD

There are several implications of these requirements for determining a diagnosis of personality disorder following deployment. Since the onset of personality disorders by definition occurs by late adolescence or early adulthood, there typically should be evidence of the behavior pattern prior to adulthood. A history of solid adjustment and good psychosocial functioning prior to adulthood would not be expected in an individual with a personality disorder.

It is critical to rule out other mental disorders that may be responsible for the maladaptive behaviors in making a clinical diagnosis of personality disorder. Following an extended event characterized by traumatic stressors, it is particularly important to determine if problematic behaviors are due to PTSD. The DSM-IV explicitly states "When personality changes emerge and persist after an individual has been exposed to extreme stress, a diagnosis of Post Traumatic Stress Disorder should be considered." Exposures to severe or prolonged trauma can result in behaviors that look like features of personality disorders. PTSD criteria include irritability or outbursts of anger, feeling of detachment or estrangement from others, and restricted range of affect (unable to experience feelings such as love). In addition, the DSM-IV describes several associated features of PTSD that may be present, including self-destructive and impulsive behavior, social withdrawal, feeling constantly threatened, and impaired relationships with others.

# Signs of PTSD

The recognition of possible personality changes following severe or prolonged stress is apparent in the International Classification of Diseases (ICD-10), which includes a diagnostic category of "Enduring personality change after catastrophic

## Screening for Personality Disorder

A soldier unfit for duty because of a PD [personality disorder] can often be identified in the training or early deployment phases of duty. Boot camp and related activities are emotionally intense and demanding crucible. As such they act as a natural "stress test," unmasking a person's innate problems with coping and impulse control—difficulties that he or she could otherwise compensate for in civilian life. Individuals' tendencies to become hostile, aggressive, resistant to authority under pressure, suspicious of others' motives, and disruptive to unit cohesion will likely assert themselves in the context of these environments, to the notice of those around including command and especially peers.

Thus, the time to intercept these individuals in order to treat or discharge them as unfit for duty, as the military deems appropriate, is at intake, during training, before they are deployed, or early in the deployment period.

*Sally Satel,*
*"Statement before House Committee on Veterans' Affairs,"*
*July 25, 2007.*

experience." This diagnosis is used in cases of persistent change in personality following extreme stress, including prolonged exposure to life-threatening situations, characterized by two or more of the following features newly present after the trauma:

1. A hostile or distrustful attitude toward the world

2. Social withdrawal

3. A constant feeling of emptiness or hopelessness

4. An enduring feeling of "being on edge" or being threatened without any external cause, as evidenced by an increased vigilance and irritability.

5. A permanent feeling of being changed or being different from others (estrangement).

These features may be present in individuals exposed to extreme trauma. Again, such features overlap with many of the criteria for Personality Disorders. The critical distinction is whether they represent change in personality following exposure to severe traumatic stress. Although I have focused here on the distinction between Personality Disorders and PTSD, it is important to recognize that these conditions can co-exist. A person able to function in spite of a mild-to moderate personality disorder can develop PTSD after trauma. An additional consideration I have not discussed is Traumatic Brain Injury, which is sometimes associated with behavioral changes that may look like features of personality disorders, for example, aggression, poor impulse control, or suspiciousness. For individuals with exposure to head injury (including closed head injury), neuropsychological testing may be indicated to rule out brain injury as a cause of such behaviors.

## Assessments at the VA

VA psychologists conduct assessments for service connected disability applications. These "compensation and pension" exams follow established guidelines, and cover psychosocial functioning and symptoms of mental disorder present prior to, during, and following military service. Military experience, including exposure to traumatic events, is assessed, and the timing of the onset of symptoms in relation to military service is determined. Most of the exams that I personally have conducted have been to establish service connection for PTSD. These require detailed questioning of symptoms of PTSD and other mental disorders, including timing of onset. If there is a pattern of maladaptive behavior existing prior to military service, it is important to determine whether there has been a change in connection with military service. Diagnoses reflect a personality disorder if present but, in my personal experience, this has been rare. As noted above, a personality disorder can also co-exist with PTSD. In my experience, these exams take about 60 minutes on average, but can take longer in more complicated cases.

Also of note is that VA policy now requires screening of all OEF/OIF [Operation Enduring Freedom/Operation Iraqi Freedom] veterans for Traumatic Brain Injury. Positive responses to the screen are followed up with more detailed assessments by neuropsychologists.

To summarize, events characterized by repeated exposure to traumatic stress can result in symptoms and behaviors that appear, on the surface, to resemble personality disorder. A clinical diagnosis of personality disorder should be made only when it can clearly be established that the behavioral patterns and associated psychosocial impairment or distress were present by late adolescence or early adulthood, existed prior to stressful events, and cannot be better explained by the experience during an event of traumatic stress or brain injury. In addition to a comprehensive psychological assessment of the individual, consultation with family members or others with knowledge of the individual prior to service is advisable when considering a personality disorder diagnosis. The significance of an accurate diagnosis cannot be underestimated.

# Periodical Bibliography

*The following articles have been selected to supplement the diverse views presented in this chapter.*

Jill Carroll | "'We're Going to Be Paying for This for a While': Soldiers Bring the War Home," *Christian Science Monitor*, January 1, 2009.

Sharon Cotliar | "Autism & Vaccines: One Family's Victory," *People*, March 24, 2008.

Conor B. McDonough | "The Mainstreaming Requirement of the Individuals with Disabilities Act in the Context of Autism Spectrum Disorders," *Fordham Urban Law Review*, October 2008.

Elizabeth Mechcatie | "New Warning OK for ADHD Drugs, But No Black Box: FDA Pediatric Panel Gives Second Opinion," *Pediatric News*, April 2006.

Anton Miller | "Special Needs Debate Doesn't Need Ideology," *Vancouver Sun*, March 5, 2007.

Paul Offit | "Autism and Vaccines—A Careless Ruling," *Dallas Morning News*, April 7, 2008.

Paul T. Shattuck and Maureen Durkin | "A Spectrum of Disputes," *New York Times*, June 11, 2007.

Stephen D. Sugarman | "Cases in Vaccine Court—Legal Battles Over Vaccines and Autism," *New England Journal of Medicine*, September 27, 2007.

Elizabeth A. Yi | "Vaccine Lawsuit Hazards," *Washington Times*, June 8, 2008.

Alison Young | "First Autism-Vaccine Link: How Hannah Made History," *Atlanta Journal-Constitution*, March 6, 2008.

# For Further Discussion

## Chapter 1

1. John Wanner and Sarah Rasher both claim to have adult attention deficit disorder. While Wanner sees the disorder as a disability, Rasher sees it as a gift. How do the life experiences of these two authors differ? Do these experiences influence their arguments? Explain why or why not, citing from both texts.

2. Anne McElroy Dachel argues that autism has increased to epidemic proportions. Lawrence Scahill disputes this claim. Identify the types of evidence each author uses to support his or her argument. Which type of evidence do you find more persuasive? Citing from the viewpoints, explain.

3. Joel Turtel disputes that ADHD is a disease. Turtel sees the behaviors said to be symptoms of this disorder as a reflection of a social malaise. How does the way society views the behaviors thought of as symptoms of ADHD influence the arguments on both sides of the debates in this chapter? What do the viewpoints on both sides of these debates have in common and how do they differ? Explain your answers, citing from the viewpoints.

## Chapter 2

1. *NewsRx Health* claims that attention-deficit/hyperactivity disorder (ADHD) stems from biological causes. Fred Baughman disputes this claim, arguing that ADHD drugs themselves may lead to brain atrophy in those with ADHD. Identify the types of evidence these authors use to support their arguments. Which type of evidence do you find more persuasive? Citing from the viewpoints, explain.

2. D.E. Ford, Jeff Huber, and I.L. Meagher argue that the number of veterans returning from Iraq with post-traumatic stress disorder is increasing. Sally Satel claims that these estimates are exaggerated. Note the authors' affiliations. Does this affiliation make their viewpoints more or less persuasive? Explain.

3. Since diseases such as autism and post-traumatic stress disorder may require long-term treatment, the costs of treatment could in many cases be significant. Do you think the cost of such treatments influences any of the viewpoints in this chapter? Citing from the text, explain why or why not.

4. Based on the principles of the scientific method and the ethical principles governing human experiments, why is it difficult to identify causes when studying behavioral disorders? What research cited by the viewpoints in this chapter suffers from this challenge? Explain.

# Chapter 3

1. Which of the treatments in this chapter do you think will be most effective in addressing behavioral disorders? To what extent, if any, is your decision based on your understanding of a disorder's causes or its severity? Explain, citing the viewpoints.

2. The Institute of Medicine discusses the problem of experimental bias in its viewpoint dismissing the effectiveness of most post-traumatic stress disorder treatments. What research on other treatments explored in this chapter might suffer from experimental bias? Explain your answer, citing from the viewpoints.

3. While Norman Sussman believes that drugs have many benefits in the treatment of attention-deficit/hyperactivity disorder (ADHD), Frank Lawlis believes that the risks of the drugs are too great. What types of evidence does each

offer to support his claim? Which type of evidence do you find more persuasive? Explain, citing from the viewpoints.

4. How does the affiliation of the authors in this chapter influence their rhetoric? Do you think this makes one viewpoint more persuasive than the other? Explain why or why not, citing from the viewpoints.

## Chapter 4

1. What do the arguments for and against the Vaccine Injury Compensation Program have in common with the arguments for and against the need for black box warnings for ADHD drugs? Explain, citing from the viewpoints.

2. Leslie Werstein Hann outlines the benefits of mainstreaming in her viewpoint. Robert Tomsho, on the other hand, cites the experience of parents who think mainstreaming does more harm than good. If it should be left to the parents to decide whether to put their autistic children in separate schools, who should bear the cost? If states cannot afford to build and maintain separate schools, how will that impact low-income parents who want to put their autistic children in separate schools? Do the viewpoints offer any guidance on these questions? Citing the viewpoints, explain.

3. Note the affiliations of the authors on both sides of the debate over personality disorder discharges among veterans. Do these affiliations make their viewpoints more or less persuasive? Explain.

4. What commonalities among the evidence and opinions can you find in the viewpoints on both sides of the debate in this chapter? What impact do these strategies have on the viewpoints' persuasiveness? Explain, citing from the viewpoints.

# Organizations to Contact

*The editors have compiled the following list of organizations concerned with the issues debated in this book. The descriptions are derived from materials provided by the organizations. All have publications or information available for interested readers. The list was compiled on the date of publication of the present volume; the information provided here may change. Be aware that many organizations take several weeks or longer to respond to inquiries, so allow as much time as possible.*

**American Academy of Child and Adolescent Psychiatry (AACAP)**
3615 Wisconsin Ave. NW, Washington, DC   20016-3007
(202) 966-7300 • fax: (202) 966-2891
e-mail: communications@aacap.org
Web site: www.aacap.org

AACAP is a nonprofit organization that supports and advances child and adolescent psychiatry through research and education. The academy's goal is to provide information that will remove the stigma associated with mental illnesses and assure proper treatment for children who suffer from mental or behavioral disorders. It publishes the monthly *Journal of the American Academy of Child and Adolescent Psychiatry* and the fact sheets "Children Who Can't Pay Attention/ADHD" and "The Child with Autism."

**American Academy of Pediatrics (AAP)**
141 Northwest Point Blvd.
Elk Grove Village, IL   60007-1098
(847) 434-4000 • fax: (847) 434-8000
Web site: www.aap.org

AAP is a professional member organization of pediatricians in the United States, Canada, and Latin America who work together to address the health needs of children. The academy publishes the monthly journal *Pediatrics*, and the monthly newsletter *AAP News*. AAP has developed the booklets "Understanding Autism Spectrum Disorders (ASD)" and "Understanding the Child with ADHD: Information for Parents About Attention-Deficit/Hyperactivity Disorder." Its Web site also includes articles and audio files with information on behavioral disorders, including "Sound Advice on Vaccines."

## American Psychological Association (APA)

750 First Street NE, Washington, DC   20002-4242
(202) 336-5500 • fax: (202) 336-5708
e-mail: public.affairs@apa.org
Web site: www.apa.org

The American Psychological Association is the largest scientific and professional organization representing psychology in the United States and is the world's largest association of psychologists. It publishes numerous books, including *Parenting Children with ADHD: Lessons That Medicine Cannot Teach*. Its Web site includes articles and congressional testimony on attention-deficit/hyperactivity disorder, autism, obsessive-compulsive disorder, post-traumatic stress disorder, and other behavioral disorders.

## Anxiety Disorders Association of America (ADAA)

8730 Georgia Ave., Suite 600, Silver Spring, MD   20910
(240) 385-1001 • fax: (240) 485-1035
e-mail: information@adaa.org
Web site: www.adaa.org

ADAA is dedicated to the prevention, treatment, and cure of anxiety disorders and to improving the lives of all people who suffer from them. It disseminates information, provides links to those who need treatment, and advocates cost-effective treatments. ADAA publishes the book *Facing Panic: Self-Help for People with Panic Attacks*, the quarterly newsletter *Triumph*, and fact sheets and brochures, available on its Web site.

## Attention Deficit Disorder Association (ADDA)

PO Box 7557, Wilmington, DE   19803-9997
(800) 939-1019 • Fax: (800) 939-1019
e-mail: adda@jmoadmin.com
Web site: www.add.org

ADDA is a national nonprofit organization whose mission is to provide information, resources, and networking to adults with ADHD and professionals working with them. It publishes the quarterly journal, *Focus*, and provides information and links about ADHD on its Web site.

## Autism Research Institute

4182 Adams Ave., San Diego, CA   92116
(619) 281-7165 • fax: (619) 563-6840
Web site: www.autism.com

This national organization focuses on research and information concerning autism and related disorders. The organization started Defeat Autism Now! (DAN!), an autism think tank and conference group, and publishes the quarterly *Autism Research Review International Newsletter*, past issues of which are available on its Web site, as are links to editorials on the topic. The Web site also publishes fact sheets and links to other autism organizations.

## Autism Society of America (ASA)

7910 Woodmont Ave., Suite 300, Bethesda, MD   20814-3067
(301) 657-0881 • fax: (301) 657-0869
e-mail: info@autism-society.org
Web site: www.autism-society.org

ASA is one of the largest autism support groups in the United States, with nearly 200 chapters. It provides information and referrals to autism services nationwide. Its mission is to increase public awareness of autism and to help individuals with autism and their families deal with day-to-day issues. Its Web site offers a free e-newsletter, *ASA-Net*.

**Autism Speaks**
2 Park Ave., 11th Floor, New York, NY 10016
(212) 252-8584 • fax: (212) 252-8676
e-mail: contactus@autismspeaks.org
Web site: www.autismspeaks.org

This national organization promotes public awareness of autism and works to fund research into the causes, prevention, and treatment of autism. Its Web site offers the *e-Speaks* newsletter, as well as news archives.

**Children and Adults with**
**Attention-Deficit/Hyperactivity Disorder (CHADD)**
8181 Professional Place, Suite 150, Landover, MD 20785
(301) 306-7070 • fax: (301) 306-7090
e-mail: national@chadd.org
Web site: www.chadd.org

CHADD is a nonprofit organization founded by a group of concerned parents that works to improve the lives of children and adults with attention-deficit/hyperactivity disorder through education, advocacy, and support. It publishes the bimonthly *Attention!* magazine, books, and many fact sheets about the disorder.

**Institute for Vaccine Safety**
Bloomberg School of Public Health
Johns Hopkins University
615 N. Wolfe Street, Baltimore, MD 21205
Web site: www.vaccinesafety.edu

The institute's mission is to provide an independent assessment of vaccines and vaccine safety to help guide decision makers and educate physicians, the public, and the media about key issues surrounding the safety of vaccines. The institute's goal is to work toward preventing disease using the safest vaccines possible. Fact sheets and recent rulings concerning the autism/vaccine link are available on its Web site.

## National Alliance on Mental Illness (NAMI)

2107 Wilson Blvd., Suite 300, Arlington, VA   22201-3042
(703) 524-7600 • fax: (703) 524-9094
e-mail: info@nami.org
Web site: www.nami.org

NAMI is a national grassroots mental health organization that seeks to eradicate mental illness and improve the lives of persons living with serious mental illness as well as the lives of their families. NAMI works through advocacy, research, education, and support. The organization publishes a magazine called *The Advocate.*

## National Autism Association (NAA)

1330 W. Schatz Lane, Nixa, MO   65714
(877) NAA-AUTISM
e-mail: naa@nationalautism.org
Web site: www.nationalautismassociation.org

NAA focuses on autism research, advocacy, education, and support for those affected by autism. Its goal is to educate society that autism is not a lifelong, incurable genetic disorder, but one that is biomedically definable and treatable. NAA also works to raise public and professional awareness of environmental toxins as causative factors on neurological damage that often results in autism or a related diagnosis. Its Web site publishes research findings, brochures, and press releases.

## National Center for PTSD

VA Medical Center (116D), 215 N. Main Street
White River Junction, VT   05009
(802) 296-5132 • fax: (802) 296-5135
e-mail: ncptsd@va.gov
Web site: www.ncptsd.org

Part of the Department of Veterans Affairs, the center conducts research and promotes education on the prevention, understanding, and treatment of PTSD. On its Web site, the center publishes articles, manuals, newsletters, handouts, and videos. The Web site also has a quick link to the PTSD Information Center, which contains in-depth information on PTSD and traumatic stress for a general audience.

### National Institute of Mental Health (NIMH)
6001 Executive Blvd., Room 8184, MSC 9663
Bethesda, MD   20892-9663
(301) 443-4513 • fax: 301-443-4279
e-mail: nimhinfo@nih.gov
Web site: www.nimh.nih.gov/healthinformation/
adhdmenu.cfm

NIMH is the federal agency concerned with mental health research. It plans and conducts a comprehensive program of research relating to the causes, prevention, diagnosis, and treatment of mental illnesses. It produces various informational publications on mental disorders and their treatment, including the booklet *Attention Deficit Hyperactivity Disorder.*

### National Vaccine Information Center (NVIC)
407 Church Street, Suite H, Vienna, VA   22180
(703) 938-0342 • fax: (703) 938-5768
e-mail: contactnvic@gmail.com
Web site: www.nvic.org

Founded by parents of children injured by vaccines, NVIC is responsible for launching the vaccine safety and informed consent movement in America in the early 1980s. NVIC is the oldest and largest consumer organization advocating the institution of vaccine safety and informed consent protections in the mass vaccination system. On its Web site, NVIC publishes fact sheets on vaccine laws and articles on informed consent, including "Vaccine Freedom of Choice."

### Obsessive Compulsive Foundation
PO Box 961029, Boston, MA   02196
(617) 973-5801
e-mail: info@ocfoundation.org
Web site: www.ocfoundation.org

The Obsessive Compulsive Foundation is an international organization that serves those who are affected by obsessive-compulsive disorder (OCD) and other related neurobiological spectrum disorders. The goals of the foundation are to give support to individuals who suffer from OCD and those who care for them, provide education and information and promote awareness, foster research to discover causes and effective treatments of these illnesses, and advocate for the needs of those affected by OCD.

# Bibliography of Books

Sue Adams

*A Book About What Autism Can Be Like.* Philadelphia, PA: Jessica Kingsley, 2009.

Peter Roger Breggin

*Brain-Disabling Treatments in Psychiatry: Drugs, Electroshock, and the Psychopharmaceutical Complex.* New York: Spring, 2008.

Penny Coleman

*Flashback: Posttraumatic Stress Disorder, Suicide, and the Lessons of War.* Boston: Beacon, 2006.

Ruth Colker

*When Is Separate Unequal? A Disability Perspective.* New York: Cambridge University Press, 2008.

Robert M. Collie

*Obsessive-Compulsive Disorder: A Guide for Family, Friends, and Pastors.* New York: Haworth Pastoral Press, 2005.

Peter Conrad

*Identifying Hyperactive Children: The Medicalization of Deviant Behavior.* Aldershot, UK: Ashgate, 2006.

Peter Conrad

*The Medicalization of Society: On the Transformation of Human Conditions into Treatable Disorders.* Baltimore, MD: Johns Hopkins University Press, 2007.

Michelle Genevieve Craske

*Origins of Phobias and Anxiety Disorders: Why More Women Than Men?* Boston: Elsevier, 2003.

Padmal de Silva    *Obsessive-Compulsive Disorder: The Facts.* New York: Oxford University Press, 2004.

Barbara Firestone    *Autism Heroes: Portraits of Families Meeting the Challenge.* Philadelphia, PA: Jessica Kingsley, 2007.

Stephen Ray Flora    *Taking America Off Drugs: Why Behavioral Therapy Is More Effective for Treating ADHD, OCD, Depression, and Other Psychological Problems.* Albany, NY: State University of New York Press, 2007.

Ross W. Greene    *Lost at School: Why Our Kids with Behavioral Challenges Are Falling Through the Cracks and How We Can Help Them.* New York: Scribner, 2008.

Roy Richard Grinker    *Unstrange Minds: Remapping the World of Autism.* New York: Basic, 2006.

Lara Honos-Webb    *The Gift of ADHD: How to Transform Your Child's Problems into Strengths.* Oakland, CA: New Harbinger, 2005.

David Kirby    *Evidence of Harm: Mercury in Vaccines and the Autism Epidemic: A Medical Controversy.* New York: St. Martin's, 2005.

Robert McNergney and Clayton Keller, eds.    *Images of Mainstreaming: Educating Students with Disabilities.* New York: Routledge, 1999.

Joel T. Nigg — *What Causes ADHD? Understanding What Goes Wrong and Why*. New York: Guilford, 2006.

Thomas G. Plante, ed. — *Mental Disorders of the New Millennium*. Westport, CT: Praeger, 2006.

Donna Satterlee Ross and Kelly Ann Jolly, eds. — *That's Life with Autism: Tales and Tips for Families with Autism*. London: Jessica Kingsley, 2006.

Robert C. Scaer — *The Body Bears the Burden: Trauma, Dissociation, and Disease*. New York: Haworth Medical Press, 2007.

Karen M. Seeley — *Therapy After Terror: 9/11, Psychotherapists, and Mental Health*. New York: Cambridge University Press, 2008.

Terri Tanielian and Lisa H. Jaycox, eds. — *Invisible Wounds of War: Psychological and Cognitive Injuries, Their Consequences, and Services to Assist Recovery*. Santa Monica, CA: RAND, 2008.

Carol Turkington and Ruth Anan — *The A to Z of Autism Spectrum Disorders*. New York: Checkmark, 2007.

Leeann Whiffen — *A Child's Journey Out of Autism: One Family's Story of Living in Hope and Finding a Cure*. Naperville, IL: Sourcebooks, 2009.

| | |
|---|---|
| Nancy D. Wiseman and Kim Painter Koffsky | *Could It Be Autism? A Parent's Guide to the First Signs and Next Steps.* New York: Broadway Books, 2006. |
| Andrew W. Zimmerman, ed. | *Autism: Current Theories and Evidence.* Totowa, NJ: Humana, 2008. |

# Index